Be the HAPPY MOM

7 Practical Steps to Create Happy Family

Dr. Sumathi Chandrasekaran

Edited by: Shivasankari Bhuvaneswaran
Cover design by: Vaishnave Vinothraj

www.mindcafechennai.com
mindcafechennai@gmail.com

INDIA • SINGAPORE • MALAYSIA

ISBN 979-8-88772-995-4

Dedicated to loving and divine soul, Velrajan. S
Thanks for all your sacrifices; that made me
what I am today.

Contents

Preface

Be The Happy Mom

Creating your happy family

Thanks for choosing my book!

Before we begin and dive into the aspects of becoming a happy mom, I would like to take some time to look back at my past and see how I came to the point of writing a book.

It was October 4, 1996, when I succumbed utterly, due to the sudden loss of my loving brother. This came as a blow as I looked up to him and had a lovable relationship with him. He always looked out for me and showered me with unconditional love. After his demise, my inner identity crisis, which I lived through in my teenage years, cropped up again.

I lost touch with my divine inner being and spiralled down to adepressed state of mind. I even took an extreme step to leave this world as it was excruciating for me to accept this loss. Fortunately, my husband was there to support me and help me realise that I have a life and an additional responsibility as a mom of two children.

As I always loved reading books, my husband took me to Landmark and asked me to choose a book. My first book was "Manifest Your Destiny" by Wayne W. Dyer. Since then, I haven't looked back in my life. It took three months to read that book, as my English got rusty. I had to use a dictionary to understand the complex concepts discussed in the book.

Being a chemistry graduate from the Women's Christian College (1988), I always took pride in my vocabulary and communication skills. After marriage in 1989, I stopped conversing in English. As a full-time homemaker,I was busy with household chores and the responsibility of caring for children, in-laws, and more.

Slowly but steadily, I regained my English vocabulary to the extent that I finished a book in a week. As days rolled by, my thirst for knowledge increased. When my husband bought a computer in 2000 for my children, I casually started using it. That is when I discovered my hidden desire to continue my education. I remember using Google to learn more about the brain(my brother passed away due to a brain tumor). That is when I got fascinated by the mind, the brain's software. My desire to explore the intricacies of the mind led me to the field of psychology.

Hailing from an orthodox family, I faced many hardships in completing my PG in psychology. In fact, I did my PG in distance education without the knowledge of my in-laws and others who were against a married woman continuing her studies. But my husband supported me throughout this process and stood strong beside me. I observed with each step that I took; my consciousness was expanding. Though I found myself sometimes in a state of helplessness, I ventured out of my comfort zone. This was possible only by my inner companion, the infinite intelligent source of energy that orchestrates more than 80 trillion cells in my body. We will learn more about this concept in the book.

I completed my Doctorate from Madras University in 2012 under the guidance of my guide, Dr. VeenaEasavaradoss, within three years of finishing my M.Phil at Presidency College. I specialized in parenting and behavioral problems of children with learning disabilities. I chose this topic to pay tribute to my brother, who had learning difficulties. The childhood vision of running an NGO was always running in the back of my mind. So, I started an NGO for women and children called Yuvathi that focuses on the mental health and social well-being of women and children. I never stopped learning. I kept enrolling in courses and seminars to enhance my knowledge and upgrade my skills.

From being a pessimistic person with very low self-esteem, I evolved into a successful psychotherapist, an International Happiness Coach, Founder of Yuvathi, and a social entrepreneur. While these achievements speak volumes about my confidence and success in my career, as a mom, I continued to face intense tribulations and challenges, which sometimes appeared to be beyond my capacity. It was a challenging phase of my life. Despite being a successful psychologist, I struggled to play the role of a mom to my two grown-up children. I then realized I needed to mend my relationship with my parents and heal internally.

While mending my relationship with my parents was the first step, it was not everything. Soon, I realized that I often felt worthless and never good enough as a mother. As this started affecting how I viewed myself and took a hit on my self-esteem, I started looking for remedies as this was not what I wanted in my life. It is not who I wanted to be as a person. All these thoughts pushed me to discover a way out of this rabbit hole I got myself into.

After several internal experiments and learnings, I could steer myself to find self-sustainable happiness within myself. I decided to share my experience and knowledge with helpless mothers who wanted to regain their status quo. It was an inner call that made me share my spiritual journey and valuable insights to all my readers who want to learn how to be a happy mom.

Acknowledgments

To my divine spiritual father, my inner source, for being my constant companion in guiding me and making me write this book.

To my mom, S. Indhubala, for her genuineness and love showered to me.

To my children, Divya and Vinothraj who has been instrumental in writing this book.

To my life partner, Chandrasekaran, for his endless emotional support and understanding throughout my married life.

To my daughter-in-law, Vaishnave Vinothraj, for her vital assistance in designing the book cover.

To my editor, Shivasankari Bhuvaneswaran, for readily accepting to edit this book at a very short notice.

To all my colleagues and friends for their encouraging and stimulating words.

Introduction

I firmly believe my divine inner being made me write this book. You have made the right choice to select this book, as the very purpose of this book is to educate mothers who are silently suffering inside, or undergoing a continuous conflict, whether or not they are good moms.

This book is about knowing how to be a happy parent rather than just being a good one. I will show you a different perspective and offer insights into a mother's role in her children's lives and how to be a happy person from within. This book is not about teaching or giving tips for parenting. It is more about honoring and celebrating a mother's role.

In the first four chapters of this book, you will get answers to most of your doubts, and we will dispel myths about a mom's role and parenting. This book is structured so that, before teaching you parenting skills, it will make you emotionally stable enough to use them. The topics discussed will give you more clarity on how to be a happy mom. By learning how your mind works, you can understand the reason for your emotional suffering and get authentic information about parenting. First and foremost, being a person is more fundamental to being a happy mom.

In the last chapter, you will learn to apply the step-by-step process to transform yourself from being a worried mom to an empowered mom who feels genuinely happy from the inside.

You need to read these chapters sequentially to ensure that you first understand the significance of being a happy mom. The new knowledge will help expand your intellect and prepare you to use parenting skills appropriately. This knowledge and skills will empower you and make you capable enough to face anything life throws your way.

I have mentioned children throughout this book to ensure uniformity, but the age may vary according to the context. A child mentioned in this book could be of any age, from a baby to an adult.

I want you to know that being a happy mom is not your ultimate destination. The natural state helps unfold the very essence of feeling worthy enough. Hence this book will be your first step towards the life journey of realizing your true self.

Chapter I

Good Mom or a Bad Mom?

Mom – Playing the Role or Living the Role?

Intentions Matter, Not Expectations!

Perfect Mom – a Dream or Reality?

Need to be the Happy Mom – the Ultimate Purpose

Chapter 1

Good Mom or a Bad Mom?

Everything good and bad comes from your own mind. To find something beyond the mind is impossible.

– Bhodhidharma

Do you know that 99 percent of mothers want to be accepted as good moms in their life? Most likely, you could be one of them. Most mothers want to be recognized not only by their children but also by society. This is a universal phenomenon that I have observed in 17 years of practice as a counseling psychologist. Most mothers have this typical question, "Am I a good mom?" running through their minds constantly when their child doesn't turn out to be successful. If you are one of them, this section is definitely for you.

As a mom, you feel the fullest joy when your children lead a happy life on their own. However, life is not always filled with sunshine and rainbows. Sometimes you have to see them dealing with unhealthy emotions or struggles. While life can initially give you joyful experiences with your child, there are chances that you will experience painful moments with the same child. What's worse, it could also become unbearable or toxic. It takes a lot of strength and courage to see your children going through hardships in their personal life. These instances eventually put a mother at crossroads resulting in an inner conflict with her helplessness to take control of the situation. That is where the self-doubt about being a good mom starts to kick in.

Let me explain why mothers are obsessed with being good moms. This belief, "I should be a good mom," is rooted deeply in the complex neural circuits of our brains (I will elaborate more in the 4th chapter). These genetically inherited beliefs will influence our actions in any given circumstance. It would be hard to digest that the thoughts unconsciously embedded in our subconscious mind decide almost all our habitual behavior. This unhealthy belief, "I should be a good mom," drives each mom to prove herself to others. Worse, women value themselves only if they are doing a good enough job as a mom. This universal belief, imprinted without awareness, affects our behavior towards children.

In reality, no mother is either a good or a bad mom. Do we label an infant as a good or a bad baby? Do we mention God/Creator as good or bad? Never! As a parent, you perceive your baby as a bundle of pure love and joy which is whole and complete. Then what stops us from seeing ourselves as a whole and complete mom? Why do you need to label yourself as a good or a bad mom? Good is an adjective that doesn't give us any helpful information regarding a parent or their actions. It is a very relative term usually used to approve something or a person in a judgmental way. Instead of striving to be a good person to seek society's approval, understand that you are already a good soul being a product of unconditional love.

Most mothers suffer from this "being perfect" syndrome. Nobody is perfect in this world. Perfection kills the process making it hard to enjoy parenthood which unfolds a beautiful, healthy relationship between you and your child. Parenting is a privilege and a responsibility; it doesn't have to be burdensome. I will take you through a journey where you can live as the ideal mom you always wanted to be in your life.

Parenting is not just a duty; it is a way of life. Rather than wondering whether a mother is good or bad, check if the parenting is good. A mother's intentions are always pure, and she always hopes for the best for her child. While mothers may be genuine in their thoughts and feelings, sometimes they may end up being harsh, hurting their child's feelings and ultimately making them feel guilty. Though they love their child unconditionally, they may sometimes find themselves in a contradictory position. The child will notice this behavior rather than a mother's true intention behind each action.

Children perceive parents as supreme beings since parents show extreme care for the child for the first seven years. Parents go out of their way to fulfill a child's physical and emotional needs. The child depends on parent's acceptance and approval to shape themselves. Only unconditional acceptance will develop a child into a healthy individual. Unfortunately, this doesn't happen for all children. Parents often find it challenging to approve or accept their children unconditionally. As a baby, it would be easy, but eventually, as they grow, it becomes tough to get them unconditionally.

To get out of this self-destructive cycle, knowing and understanding how your mind prevents you from being a happy mom is imperative. God has endowed us with a powerful instrument called the mind, yet most of us are unequipped or unaware of using it well. The first step in unlocking the potential of this dynamic tool is seal-realization.

As a mom, I often ask myself these questions. Did my parents adequately train me to face stressful situations? Was I taught how to keep myself emotionally stable during challenging times in my life? Did my parents show me how to keep myself happier and joyful irrespective of what goes on in life? Are my past experiences valuable in some way in the present world situation? My answers to all these questions imply that I could only give what I have received. Stressful parents create stressful and unhappy children. A mindful mom has a mind that is happier and more peaceful. How many of us are living in the present moment? How many of us can stay calm and stable in challenging situations? These are the questions we need to ask ourselves to take complete ownership of our life.

I am a mom of two young adults. My elder daughter is married and has 2 children—they reside in Dubai. My son is married to a fantastic daughter-in-law who lives with us. As a mom of two grown-up adults and a grandmother of 2 children, I experience a variety of emotional conflicts on a day-to-day basis. When my daughter was born in 1990, I was promoted to the mom position. It is a moment I cherish as it gave me a unique, joyful experience.

The moment I became a mom, I decided to give her the best of everything I had, along with the confidence to be herself. I was an experimental mom trying to follow parenting books to the tee. Whether it was about choosing the perfect dress, giving her nutritional food, or enrolling her in the school, I ensured that it was the best. What made me so particular about giving her the best in everything? It was my poor self-image.

Since my childhood, I always felt that I was not treated the way I deserved to be treated. My mom showered her love in her own way, but it was inconsistent. I never experienced unconditional love. This void was wide open in my heart till the age of 30. My mom later told me that she believed that I was an unworthy girl.

When my mom was carrying me in her womb, at nine months, my father had an accident that damaged one of his legs. Doctors told him that he could never walk again and the chances of it happening were minimal. But fortunately, he started to walk with sheer determination and willpower. Some of the relatives made my mom believe that the unborn child's bad luck made them undergo this difficulty.

An infant in the womb will be affected by the emotional status of its mother. My innocent mother believed my arrival into this world brought bad luck to my dad. This emotional distress of my mom had a huge emotional impact on me in the final month.

It took me years to realize how the emotional distress of my mom had affected my self-worthiness. I had moments of happiness and exhilaration with my precious daughter, as well as moments of emotional outbursts. Unfortunately, when I found it difficult to handle my daughter, I labeled myself as a bad mom, which was untrue. This was a universal trap that most mothers suffer from. I never realized my hardships until a life-changing event when I was 29 years old, in 1996. I will discuss it in detail in the upcoming chapters.

Through my journey in life, I realized my life's purpose and it helped me transform from being a sad person to a happy individual from within. I am a logical person, who has a scientific bent of mind. I will share my knowledge and professional expertise and the unique insights that made me the person I am today. This book will help you regain your power as a mom and realize the essence of feeling worthy of yourself.

Mom – Playing the Role or Living the Role?

You play multiple roles, including a wife, sister, mom, aunt, friend,mother-in-law, grandmother, and more. The most significant and pivotal role is the role of a mom to your children as it impacts all other areas of your life.

Playing a role and living a role are not one and the same. How attached you are to that particular role decides the strength of your relationship. You start to live the role when you get connected to a role. Every role is temporary and short-lived in that particular context. During your childhood, the role of a student would be your predominant role, after which it may take a minor role. You will take on more roles at every stage of your life. Some of these roles could be a burden sometimes, as they may come with more responsibilities.

Moreover, in each role, you will observe the reflection of the self-identity that you hold inside. Your self-image is a collection of beliefs about yourself that you have formed from all your emotional experiences with your parents, teachers, friends, relatives, siblings, and society. Among these, the most significant are your parents. In the first 7 years of life, the prefrontal cortex in your frontal lobe, the conscious mind, is not fully developed, so you can't discriminate between what is good and bad for you.

For example, if you are in a teaching profession, you may expect strict adherence from your students. You are so emotionally involved with the teacher/lecturer role that you may sometimes enact that position even to your family members. When I started practicing as a psychologist, I began to identify myself more as a psychologist than in any other role I played.

Mothers are always expected to be loving, sacrificing, and patient in our society. This is rather taxing for a mom who finds it difficult to balance her own emotional needs and the parenting role. As we grow, we tend to copy our parent's behavior unconsciously, which will permanently be imprinted on our subconscious minds. Those memories with our parents get etched as neural pathways called beliefs with corresponding emotions.

For example, if you notice your mom shouting at you for disobedience,you may end up shouting at your children when they don't obey. Our lives are determined by the beliefs that are stored in our subconscious minds. When an autocratic or controlling parent raises you, you will internalize their behaviors and emotions with non-verbal cues.

The parental voice will become the inner critic inside your head, ultimately influencing your parenting style in any situation. That is how most of us end up just like our mom or dad when we did not want to be like them. The same holds true for any parenting style. It is observed that this inner critic, the internalized inner parent, could affect your other roles also. If you play a role of a wife or boss, the way you treat others may be controlling or dominating in most situations. If you can be conscious or mindful about yourself, you may be able to play the role and not live the role.

I was more influenced by my mom than my dad, as I spent the most time with her. She always (even now) insists I obey her instructions or listen to what she says, and I should never talk back. This was very difficult for me. Every time I rebelled against her authority, I will be controlled or punished by her. This affected my self-esteem a lot. When I became a mom, I told myself I would never hit my children and would be very kind to them. To my dismay, I found myself becoming my mom's mini version. I was demanding obedience, and sometimes when frustrated, I would hit my children. This had a significant impact later in both my life and that of my children.

We all want to experience peace, love, and happiness in our life. This is undeniable. Why does everyone want it? If we look closer, we will know that we are more comfortable with joy than despair or sadness. Whatever feels comfortable to us is our true nature.

Once we realize our true nature, we will not identify ourselves with the beliefs that we carry in our subconscious minds. When I realized this, I started setting clear intentions. I wanted to be a joyful mom rather than a helpless and sad mom. I detached myself from labeling myself as good or bad. Being a loving person is more important than being a good mother or wife. This shifted my perspective entirely and helped me affirm my way of being more kind and empathetic to my children. It helped me to transform from a helpless mom to a lovable (unconditional) mom, what my children expected from me.

If your intentions are unclear, you will lose control over your actions, and your relationship will become a problem. It's essential to set clear intentions before having expectations for your children. In the next section, I will discuss how selecting the right intention matters while raising children.

Intentions Matter, Not Expectations!

As a mom, your intention may be very loving and caring to your children, but you may end up shouting or threatening your child, which is the polar opposite. This is the greatest challenge that every mom faces when raising a child. When you want to give your best to your children, but start realizing that your good intentions don't impact parenting. Why does this happen? How can you resolve this?

As a mom, you may constantly worry about doing things the right way; instead, focus on what kind of mother you want to be to your children. This ritual of intentionally choosing what type of mother you want to be, irrespective of how your child behaves, will help you to stay focused. Don't expect the child to always be obedient or understanding because it is external and not under your control. Anything external is not under your control, whereas everything internal is under your control. Let's classify what is external and what is internal. How people treat you, how your child behaves, or what others think or feel about you are superficial. However, how you perceive something or respond to a situation is entirely under your control and is internal.

These intentions are governed by you and can make you feel powerful and put you in control. Your inner power is minimized when you try to shift the blame on others or the situation. You unknowingly give the power away by not taking ownership of the feelings you experience. Instead of feeling like a victim, you could choose to feel powerful by taking ownership of your actions.

These intentions will help you respond positively to your child regardless of stressful situations.

It also helps build your self-esteem, as you don't rely on others or your child to feel good. For example, when your child throws tantrums or your teenage child is not studying, you may focus on their actions and not expect them to behave in a particular way. So, instead of being reactive and shouting at them, you will choose to remain calm and responsive.

I remember vividly when my elder brother, aged 30, passed away due to a brain tumor in 1996. I was married and was a mother of two children. I was just 29 years old. I didn't have the intellectual capacity or awareness to understand what was happening in my life. I was so innocent that I blindly believed whatever others told me. I was a chemistry graduate who was a full-time homemaker, as I had to take care of my two children. My brother loved me and was caring and protective of me. I did not have a close relationship with my dad as he could not spend much time with me. I had idolized my brother as my dad. I had never felt loved and accepted by both mom and dad. My mom always expected me to stay calm and obey whatever she said. This was a complex challenge for me because I was a rebel. I constantly asked her questions that made her uncomfortable.

When I was in 3rd standard, my mom gave me an expensive scented eraser. She told me to keep it carefully for at least one month. As usual, I misplaced it. So the next day, I was given half an eraser to school. At school, I had a friend whom I liked very much. He cut my eraser into small bits and put it in my box, after which my mom denied me even the half eraser. I was given a quarter portion of the eraser, which made me feel so inadequate that I started believing I was a careless girl. My mom did not have clear intentions on what kind of mom she wanted to be, and it affected

the process of building a healthy relationship. She was more focused outside on the expectation she had of me. She wanted me to be more careful and responsible. However, she could not convey her intentions to me. Why? She was more focused on my mistakes. My mom's intention was not to punish me, but her misplaced idea was that her strict actions would change me.

How many of you know that you can change your child's behavior only with their permission and consent? Maybe, before your child is 6 years you can make them do what you want. But after those formative years, they start to think independently and possess the discretion to follow or dismiss your instructions. I decided to rebel as it was my personality trait. What's more, each of us is surrounded by a bio-electromagnetic field. This field is unique to everyone. This phenomenon is utilized in modern gadgets, where we use thumb impressions to lock/unlock our mobiles. Your brain controls this bio-electromagnetic energy field. Without the permission of your mind, no one can interrupt your energy.

In any relationship, your intention is an emotional GPS and helps you achieve what you want. When you have expectations, you tend to get disappointed or annoyed. These emotions will subsequently affect your behavior towards your child. When you set an intention of how you want to be and clearly define the purpose of your actions, you will feel more organized. For example, if I set my intention to be a loving mom, then in any situation, I will never blame my child for what I feel.

Did you know? Your feelings are a result of a chemical reaction in consequence of the thoughts in your mind. Emotions are energy in motion—the release of certain neuro-chemicals that keep circulating in your body. These neuro-chemicals drive you to behave in a particular way in response to a situation. Happy neuro-chemicals, like dopamine, oxytocin, serotonin, and endorphins (DOSE), make you feel good and make your actions productive and valuable. The exact opposite happens when stress neurochemicals are released. Only by being conscious and clear of your intentions, even in a very stressful situation, will you feel sadness but not get depressed. While you may get annoyed, you will not dwindle into anger. You can express your concern appropriately without getting anxious. And, best of all, your unrealistic fear will be replaced by awareness. When you feel appropriate feelings, you can take charge of the situation and use your intellectual capacity to act more rationally.

This doesn't demand you to become a perfect mom. One of the primary reasons why most moms are stressed is the gap between who they want to be and who they currently are. Most importantly, the need to be perfect has become the primary reason for stress. The following section concerns whether being an ideal mom is a myth or a reality.

Perfect Mom – a Dream or Reality?

What is the need to be perfect in the first place? This need has been fuelled since your childhood days. Essentially, you are perfect on a spirit level. Bob Proctor claims that "Your spiritual DNA is perfect." Inside us is a spiritual presence, a non-physical self that yearns to expand and exceed all constraints and limitations. In a self-aware state, you can feel the creative self within, and it will always try to communicate and connect with you. Your egotistical self and the cluttered mind may inhibit or restrain your connection with this expansive intelligence hidden inside you. While ego by itself is not unhealthy, it is not an evolving part of you. Your spiritual DNA is perfect as a spiritual being, meaning your identity embodies your potency, gifts, passion, and inner calling. When I started my self-discovery journey 20 years back, I realized my potential and my passion. Later, when I had my inner calling, I learned how to contribute and serve the betterment of humanity.

This spiritual energy of perfectness is why everyone feels the need to be perfect in whatever they do. On the other side, you strive toward being perfect to compensate for your sense of inadequacy. Consider this; we are living in three levels of consciousness—the physical(body), intellectual(mind), and spiritual(energy). It is acceptable to feel imperfect at the physical level and okay to feel perfect at the spiritual level.

In day-to-day life, it's common for mothers to be described as superwomen who multitask regularly. What I mean by multitasking is a mother who can prepare dinner while loading clothes in the washing machine while holding her kid on the hip and answering the doorbell, or making and receiving phone calls. However, several studies show that multitasking could harm a mother's mental health. Moreover, multitasking moms are liable to depression compared to their counterparts who let things slide. Multitasking also takes longer to finish tasks and leaves room for errors.

According to the American Psychological Association (APA), doing multiple things in swift succession can reduce output or efficiency by nearly 40 percent. That is because switching from one chore to another makes it hard to ignore distractions, impairs intellectual ability, and creates mental blocks that can slow you down. To substantiate this, a study by Clifford Nass, a Stanford University scholar, found that continuous streams of information from several sources harm the brain's health. Because all the exercise drains sugar from the brain, making the brain less equipped to perform tasks. The study established that multitasking made people inferior at extracting relevant information from irrelevant details.

Females are not endowed with supernatural powers to play different roles simultaneously. Undeniably, women are hardwired to be more resilient and prevailing as they are the stronger sex. Before you have the time to feel outraged, let me explain my statement. According to Dr. Fasih, the X chromosome is genetically proven to have more affinity towards stronger immunity and cancer prevention than the Y chromosome. We all know that women have double the amount of X chromosomes. Furthermore, she states that if a female and a male baby are born preterm, there is a higher chance of survival of the female child because of the strong resilience and survival instinct.

To substantiate this, the woman is the one who carries another life for nine months in her womb, whereas a man's contribution stops with his sperm. So women are hardwired to carry enough strength—physiologically, psychologically, and emotionally to weather the stress of pregnancy. It is said that with every childbirth, a woman gives away 50 percent of her nutritional store—reserves of iron, calcium, phosphorus, etc. to build a life within her. But after the child is born, the estrogen helps her bounce back. It helps develop her strength, resilience, and nutrition from scratch, and everything gets replenished. This proves the power of her endurance and agility. This innate endowment in a woman helps in times of crisis when she can act with her head and heart, making her physically and emotionally ready to protect her family. The men are traditionally hunter-gatherers who can go out and procure but have trouble multitasking or generally being available emotionally.

Now that I have adequately explained my statement, let us return to the topic at hand: parenting. In my opinion, the two most important things every parent needs to make the child feel are you are okay and you are loved. This is essential for your child to become a healthy individual. As a mom, realize that your child need not be perfect to be accepted by you. You need to make your child believe they were born as lovable beings and will breathe their last breath being loved. But the intermediate period of growing up is what alters everything. That is where the role of parents and the environment quality steps in and determines a child's journey between his/her life and death.

Hence a mom must be stable and happy to ensure the child grows into a healthy adult. The following section is about your need to be a happy mom and its significance.

Need to be the Happy Mom – the Ultimate Purpose

Being happy always is an unrealistic goal as it is impossible to be 100 percent happy, especially for a mom. Most of you know that happiness is a state of mind and an internal process. Achieving or finding happiness should not be your intention; instead, your focus should be on aligning your thoughts and feelings with your core values. Instead of searching outside, allow the happiness to unfold from within you. As bliss is true human nature, it will drive you to find happiness in everything. All your actions and behavior will help achieve peace and happiness within you.

> ***Everything you see, hear, taste, smell, and feel is temporary pleasure, not the real joy you want to experience. It is not wrong to experience pleasure, but if left unsupervised by your intellect, it can lead to a state of addiction.***

You may often expect something to happen externally to feel happy. For example, your brain is conditioned to believe that you will be happy if you go to a movie. It doesn't stop there and continues within every one of us. You may think if I get this job I will be happy or if my child studies well I will be happy and if my child eats healthy food I will be satisfied. The list just goes on and on. Whatever you experience through your five senses is felt as sensations in your body. These sensations are interpretations of your mind. If your mind is not calm and organized, you may perceive stress, even in simple situations. Only when your mind is still and peaceful can you observe and perceive accurately. The foundation to building a good relationship with your child requires deep faith and trust.

The essential ingredient in any relationship is feeling safe and secure. Your child must feel safe and secure with you while growing up. That's when they start to trust you, as you always ensure that they are fed, dressed, protected, and comfortable. This is how trust builds in a relationship. Trust is knowing that they feel secure and accepted for who they are. However, you cannot hold yourself responsible for your children's emotions. The best thing you can do for your kids is to keep your mind safe and sound to offer emotional support to your child whenever they need it.

If you could only trust one person, it should be yourself. Most of us relate to trust by having certain expectations and tend to get upset for not living up to our expectations. When you are the best version of the mom you can be, your child will thrive in their life rather than merely survive.

People often tend to confuse trust with expectations. Let's assume that you lend your friend some money. For the first two times, they pay it back properly. But the third time, they missed their commitment. Do you get a wave of self-righteous anger that they broke their promise to you? Instead of blaming the other person, try to draw a boundary around yourself.

You can achieve anything and everything through your mind. Knowing and understanding how your mind works are essential to being a happy mom. When you love a person, you will trust them. The more you feel safe and happy, the better you will be at all your roles.

By learning to use your mind effectively and efficiently, you can be the mom you love to be. In the following chapter, you will learn the different parts of the mind, its neuroscience, and how to use the power of the subconscious mind to achieve what and who you want to be.

POINTS TO PONDER:

1. The belief that "I should be a good mom," is rooted deeply in the complex neural circuits of our brains and that's why most mothers are obsessed with being good moms.
2. Playing a role and living a role are not one and the same. How attached you are to that particular role decides the strength of your relationship.
3. While expectations lead to hurt or disappointment, setting an intention of how you want to be and clearly defining the purpose of your actions can make you feel more stable and relaxed.
4. The spiritual energy of perfectness within is why everyone feels the need to be perfect in whatever they do.
5. A mom must be emotionally stable and happy to ensure that her children grow into healthy adults.

* * *

Chapter II

Happy Mind, Happy Mom, Happy Family

Know the Power of Your Mind

A Wandering Mind is an Unhappy Mind

Suffering is a Choice

Training Your Mind – the Key Factor for Happiness

Who Controls Your Life: You or Your Mind?

Chapter 2

Happy Mind, Happy Mom, Happy Family

Everything is energy. And that's all there is to it. Match the frequency of the reality you want and you cannot help but get that reality. It can be no other way. This is not philosophy. This is physics."

– Albert Einstein

You are a luminous being who jumped into your mom's womb with a purpose to serve and contribute to the evolution of this universe with the guidance and power of infinite intelligence within you. Unfortunately, you forgot yourself in the worldly presence of chaos and confusion. It is essential to know that you are connected universally via your super conscious mind, which is the quantum field. Based on the quantum field of science, it is said that you have the power to co-create and live your dream.

You are living in two worlds simultaneously. One is the physical world you observe, and another is the non-physical quantum inner world within you. The mind that operates your inner world is far more complex than you can imagine. The inner world hidden deep inside you is not entirely conscious. This inner world includes your evolutionary memories, past memories stored in your subconscious mind, continuous mind chatter, internal relationship, self-image, and self-talk. If this inner world is peaceful, devoid of conflicts, irrational beliefs, and negative emotions, you are in a better position to respond to any situation in the outer world. It is well-known that the external world will always throw some challenge or the other that threatens your mind. The only way to face this world full of challenges is to be mentally and emotionally prepared to respond from a resourceful state of being.

Do you find yourself focusing on the downturns and unfavourable aspects of life? That is not your fault. God has designed and wired our brains for negativity. Let me explain this further, you are endowed with a part of a brain called the reptile brain (Brain Stem). The reptile brain is 7.5 billion years old and primarily aims to protect you from danger. Your mind absorbs 11 million pieces of information per second. 10 million what you see, one million what you touch, 1 lakh is what you hear and smell, 1 thousand is what you taste. Since it's too overpowering, it condense the 11 million into 40 bits per seconds through the process of deliberate filtering and sorting. The first way, it does by is looking out for threat, or danger or anything new, as we are naturally wired to look for negativity. This is called negativity bias. This is because of pre historic conditioning. Maybe it was helpful when you lived in a dense jungle full of animals and predators that could attack you anytime. The reptile brain, the unconscious part of your mind, serves the purpose of facing any imminent danger and helps you to survive. Now in this modern world, do you need it, or is it necessary? The answer is both yes and no. No, it is not necessary, as you are now in a world where you are safe enough with a family structure and other facilities to protect yourself. Yes, it is necessary to safeguard yourself from any real danger. Whenever you try to come out of the comfort zone or break a negative pattern, your mind gives negative instructions. This is why, as a mom you may find it difficult to go beyond your environment and think good for yourself and your children.

The second way, mind filters by looking into your needs, wants or desire. It looks for what you really want or what you are constantly telling to it or what you are grateful for. This is the reason you need to be know clearly what you want and who you want to be in life.

Most of you currently perceive challenging situations and troublesome people as the real danger in your day-to-day life. This survival instinct makes your life more miserable. Hence, you need a magnificent power far greater than you to overcome this fixation on the survival mode and move towards the evolutionary model. This chapter is about empowering you with knowledge and skills to expand your intellect and propel you in the right direction.

Intellect is an integral part of the conscious mind which is present only in the human race. Intellect alone is insufficient to have a healthy relationship with your child and become a happy mom. You must understand how your mind works to unlock its total capacity and become the best version of yourself. The only thing that stands between you and what you want to be in life is your mind. When your mind is stable, peaceful, and happier irrespective of any situation, you function in your day-to-day life confidently and happily. Subsequently, you will also feel good about yourself, reinforcing your self-image and self-confidence.

You want a relationship with your child that will be closer and healthier. A happy mom will not only focus on the family's welfare and its happiness but also cherish her own emotions. Only a happy mind can help you to be a happy mom. The following section will discuss all about the mind, its parts, functioning, how to utilize its power, and how to make it your friend to be a happy mom.

Know the Power of Your Mind

Your mind is unlimited and expands beyond your physical body. Your mind is neither an object nor an entity. And it is a virtual mental space. The mind is unseen and invisible; it is not concrete like your body. Often, your mind might seem untameable. You are neither your mind nor your body; those are just two powerful tools God has given us. You are the incredible energy source that sustains and permeates beyond your mind and body.

The mind operates on three levels, namely conscious, subconscious, and super conscious. The conscious mind is your thinking mind, whereas the subconscious mind is your emotional mind. The super conscious mind is the one that exists above the level of the conscious and subconscious mind.

Your mind is like a monkey, as it has two qualities of a monkey. One is imitation, and another is jumping around (wandering). Man created this whole world through this powerful mind tool called imagination. Whatever man imagined, it became a reality. But then chaos ensued, so God gave a filter called the conscious mind. This conscious mind is the gateway that filters everything that enters or goes out of your mind.

The conscious mind is also called the educative mind or intellectual mind. We use the conscious mind while talking, walking, writing, speaking, or doing other activities. The conscious mind has so much more, like intellect, perception, imagination, reasoning, memory, and intuition. This conscious mind occupies the frontal lobe (Prefrontal Cortex), whose function varies from the subconscious mind.

The subconscious mind is also called the programmed mind or the habitual mind. The subconscious mind is the one that predominantly occupies our brain. It occupies 90 to 95 percent of the brain and its processing speed is 1 million times more than the conscious mind. The conscious mind can process only a minuscule amount of information when compared to the subconscious mind. The subconscious mind's frequency is higher than the conscious mind as thoughts are more concrete than emotions. Emotions are really energy in motion. Deep down at the subconscious level is the primitive mind (reptile brain), which helps you to survive in any situation. When you face stress, you use this part of the subconscious mind to either fight (argue/indulge in a power struggle), take flight (embrace avoidance), or merely freeze (resort to submission).

Today's neuro scientist believe that 95 percent of your brains activity is unconscious, implying that the most of the decisions you make, the way you behave, emotions you feel, depend on the 95 percent of brain activity that is beyond your conscious awareness. The subconscious mind is like a vast memory bank. It is a repository of all your experiences which are stored as memories. This mind develops in three ways. The first is completely natural, including all your genetic and physiological conditioning, such as your breathing, digestion, metabolism, excretion, etc. This happens without your conscious effort. The second way is nurturing, which encompasses all environmental forces. They may include your parents, caregivers, teachers, siblings, relatives, friends, school, social media, and political and economic conditions. All your deep-rooted beliefs (ancestors, parents) and emotional experiences are stored in the subconscious mind. Thirdly, with the help of your conscious mind with activities like learning new skills, experimenting with new ideas, creating new thoughts, and experiences you program the subconscious mind.

Although the conscious mind constitutes only 5 to 7 percent of the brain, it is the gateway to your subconscious mind. The conscious mind is the awareness mind and can process information through your 5 senses. This conscious mind can process only 50 bits of data per second compared to the 11 million bits per second processed by the subconscious mind. The subconscious mind's capacity and high processing speed are significant reasons why it is considered more powerful than the conscious mind. The conscious mind develops fully around 6 to 7 yrs. That is when your child establishes control over their body and this crucial time is when they start developing the frontal part of their brain called the neocortex.

So, until your child's conscious mind is developed, you care for their physical and emotional needs. Once their conscious mind develops and your child starts to analyze and think rationally, you gradually withdraw. You no longer need to protect or control them as they can now care for themselves. After 7 years, your children can think and make their own decisions. By the time they reach the age of 12 or 13, your child has developed most of the beliefs and their self identity starts to form. In their teenage years, they get a clarity of who they are, identify their areas of interest, discover their hidden talents, and learn social skills. Unfortunately, most children may not develop a positive self-image due to poor parenting styles and other environmental factors. As a mom, you can influence and inspire your children but never attempt to control them. You can only mitigate any problem by taking charge of your mind and not your child (except for the first 6 years of the child, when their conscious mind is not developed fully).

Your child (as a teenager) creates their self-image from all the information and experiences that are stored as memories in their subconscious mind. The irony is, before they could think rationally, they have started to picture themselves in a particular way based on how others (parents) see them. Sometimes, your child will build a self-image based on what you expect out of them and not what they think of themselves. By the time they hit 13, their full-blown mind is so powerful. Some children are so overwhelmed by their negative and positive emotions that they fail to properly channel them, and it ends up doing more harm than good in the long run. As your child steps into adolescence, they should learn to utilize their mind correctly. Unfortunately, if you are mentally stressed and unprepared to handle this change and guide them during this phase, the relationship with your child will become more complex.

From my observations, most parents face problems only when their children reach puberty. As your child is already undergoing an identity crisis, any added stress or reactive behavior from your side will impact your relationship. You must know whether your presence is contributing to their despair or happiness. If your mind wanders, you can neither focus on the present moment nor guide them appropriately. You can find true happiness only in the present moment. Therefore if your mind wanders, you will lose your happiness. We will have a detailed discussion on this topic in the next section.

A Wandering Mind is an Unhappy Mind

Your mind is always listening whenever you speak to yourself or others. As your mind hears, it forms an impression (grooves) in your subconscious mind. Only when you make an effort will your conscious mind and intellect raise questions. Without your conscious mind in play, any thought of interruption or questioning will never seep into your subconscious mind. As a result, your body will be left at the mercy of your subconscious mind, which constitutes over 95 percent of the brain.

Remember those bouts of helplessness you feel occasionally? What happens when your subconscious mind is in charge of your physical body. When you feel helpless, you either try a plausible excuse for your emotions or blame others. This tendency to shift the onus on others or a circumstance can quickly become a habit. You may have trouble taking complete responsibility for your thoughts and actions.

Being conscious of what you say, talk, and even think is imperative. If you are not mindful of your thoughts, your subconscious mind may take over the primary role of running your life. You are unaware of things imprinted inside your subconscious mind. You may have a question about why allowing the subconscious brain to take over is dangerous. It is because the stored memories of the past could be either helpful or not. For example, let us assume that one of your memories is a strong belief that you are a careless mom, which could affect how you behave with children. Naturally, you will be careless with your child, which will only strengthen your neural pathways by establishing a solid pattern.

The external world is a reflection of your inner world. While you live in the same world as others and face similar circumstances, you respond from your inner experiences. How you perceive an incident determines the emotions you experience. And, you interpret any given event based on the patterns or emotions imprinted in your subconscious mind. The thought process that happens in your inner world decides your behavior. So unless you consciously choose what to think and feel, your subconscious will take over, and you may do something you detest. When you do something you despise, its consequences can be anywhere from mild to devastating, and it is not something you would want in your life. You need to operate from your superconscious mind, and to do that, you must subdue and cross internal barriers, the mental programs in your subconscious mind. These mental programs, which are unconscious thought patterns or beliefs, might put you in a threatening mode and prevent you from behaving like the mom you want to be. Once your conscious mind is tied to your subconscious mind, you start to operate from the superconscious mind, the most potent and natural state.

Distraction is truly toxic for our well-being. According to Richard Davidson's research, 47 percent of people are not paying attention to what they are doing, and most of the time, they are in autopilot mode (subconscious mind). The conscious mind is your focus mode. When your mind wanders, you are not fully aligned with the present moment. During such instances, you won't use your conscious mind to create new thoughts or turn negative thoughts into supportive ideas. Rather than operating in autopilot mode, you need to choose your thoughts carefully so that they are aligned with the outcome you want. Only in the focus mode will you be aware of what you think and feel within. This will help you align your thoughts and emotions with the result you want to achieve. If you want your child to complete a task, think along these lines "My child is capable and competent", "I am confident that my child will accomplish this". These thoughts will make you feel confident and happy about your child and yourself. This will, in turn, determine your action towards your child.

You can get the intended results only when your thoughts, emotions, and actions are aligned. Faith is the best way to minimize your thinking mind and surpass the desire in your subconscious mind. You don't make things happen. Your job is to align your inner self with your desired outcome. Making things happen is up to the universe. Is it difficult to connect? Let me explain what I do; it would be easier to interpret. I always ensure that I give my best efforts and trust that good things manifest. This practice puts me in a faith state and makes me feel secure and satisfied. Desired results come from the state of security and faith.

I wanted to become a doctor in my childhood. As a teenager, I was neither confident nor an optimist. I mainly operated in autopilot mode. When I got 87 percent in my 12th standard board exams, I was quite disappointed as it was insufficient to get into medicine. When my cousin, a medical student at Stanley College, asked me to try medicine, my mom and dad did not let me pursue that line of work. I am not blaming my parents here, as I also

made a conscious decision at that time. My mind was filled with thoughts of self-doubt "Can I read and understand big books?," "Am I capable enough to do medicine?" If you look closely, you will notice that my thoughts were unhelpful, and naturally, I was feeling doubtful and a little anxious. Although I wanted to become a doctor, these negative emotions and mental programs prevented me from assertively expressing my thoughts to my parents. In fact, my mom told me that if I become a doctor, I will misplace the scissors in my patient's stomach. Her words insinuated indirectly that I am a careless and irresponsible girl. I remember myself laughing along with everyone. My thoughts were unsupportive and misaligned. My thoughts determine my destiny. If I cannot love and support myself, no one can ever do it for me.

The next section is understanding the purpose of suffering and how it affects the relationship with your children.

Suffering is a Choice

Why do we suffer? We suffer because we misuse two higher faculties of the conscious mind–imagination and memories. God endowed us with these two gifts to live a pleasant life, but we do the exact opposite. We let our imagination run wild and use it to think of the worst possible outcome to any situation. And rather than recollecting positive memories, our mind tends to dwell on the negative ones longer than necessary. And, so we weave ourselves into a web of suffering.

There are two types of suffering we usually go through. It is either physically at the body level or mentally at the mind level. How do we suffer physically? Some examples of physical suffering are wounds, pain, or any damage caused to your body. Mind-level suffering is the continuous, uninterrupted negative thoughts that run in your mind without direction causing chaos and confusion. This restlessness makes you feel like a victim caught in a web of negative emotions causing suffering. Positive emotions will make you feel safe and satisfied. At the same time, negative emotions make you feel insecure, drained, and unhappy. If you experience negative emotions often, irrespective of the reason, you may suffer unnecessarily.

In my teens, I wanted to become a doctor for two reasons. One, my cousin was studying medicine, and other, I would mostly fall sick due to my low immunity. Whenever I thought of becoming a doctor, I felt an immediate surge of fear. At that age, I was subjected to suffering with little knowledge and awareness. Perhaps, it was the burden of studying huge books or the self-doubt about my capability. If only I had pushed those negative thoughts aside, I might not have feared choosing medicine. You will not fear suffering when you look beyond your body and mind. The only obstacle that keeps us back is the pain in our body and mind. Once you realize that you have the choice to choose how you want to think and feel, irrespective of the situation, you stop suffering. When I wanted to do a Ph.D. in psychology in my forties, I used my will to think consciously and affirm that I would complete my doctorate within 3 years. Instead of letting my fear rule me, I shifted to a confident state of mind. When I changed my thoughts, I changed my feelings. My feelings drove me to take necessary action.

Suffering denotes that your mind is not in the present moment. As a mom, you may have early imprints of bitter incidents that you often recall or suppress unconsciously. What you don't realize is that when you bury things, they tend to be more painful. These memories become your darker side of yourselves which is stored deep inside, but more often than not, they may reflect in your own child. When you try to find the root of this darker side, you will be surprised to know that it was never your fault. The darker side you try to suppress is like a shadow lurking within you.

As a child growing up, I observed my mom as a victim who often looked helpless or frustrated. And I was expected not to express my anger in any way. My mom told me that I would be accepted by her only if I stayed obedient and calm. I unconsciously repressed my anger and other negative emotions to get her approval. Later in my life, I had difficulties expressing my anger after getting married. Instead, I was very comfortable feeling sad about everything. I had trouble dealing with anger issues, as I disliked my angry teen self. Whatever we hate within will be reflected in the outside world. In my life, the suppressed part of me was mirrored in my daughter, whom I disliked whenever she displayed anger. I was suffering unnecessarily by resisting this part, which was painful and uncomfortable. I realized that I was having a power struggle not with my daughter but with my unprocessed inner child, anger. That part was expressed as sadness inside me, which led to my depression later on.

Suffering is all about, putting you in distress or victim mode when faced with life challenges. Suffering is inevitable in this world. I have noticed that most mothers are not aware that they suffer inside. It is imperative to know how to recognize and stop your suffering. Only then can you be emotionally independent in any situation you face with your children.

It is human nature to depend on your children after a certain age. When they don't meet your expectations, you get upset or angry. Gradually, this becomes a pattern and a habitual interaction between both of you. A relationship that was once a beautiful one when your child was a baby has changed now. Why? It is not because of your child; it arises from your mismatched expectations. This is where you start to depend on your children for your happiness, as you have conditioned your mind by repeated patterns of interactions. Only with awareness can you break this pattern and respond to your child in the present moment. Ask yourself, "Do I want to be a source of strength or weakness to my children?" The obvious choice is being a source of strength. I mean that your presence as a mom needs to make your child happy, not make them feel bad about themselves. If you cry or get distressed when your child is not performing, it means your child is quickly becoming your source of weakness. Similarly, if your child is not doing well, you are serving as a source of weakness for them. It is very important that in any relationship, the person who is in awareness realizes this truth.

I had a labrador dog, Zack, for nearly 8.5 years; he was very loving and adorable. Recently on March 15, he passed away in front of me. When my dog, Zack passed away after a battle of two weeks with chronic kidney disease, I was totally disturbed. While grieving his loss, I realized that I could not control my overflowing tears and felt completely miserable. Before returning to work, I wanted to process my emotions gently and slowly so I could be involved in my work. I didn't expect to be so depressed over his loss. That is when I asked myself if I am crying constantly, does this imply that Zack is a source of pain or weakness to me? This was an enlightened thought at that moment. Immediately, I stopped crying and tried to make sense of the unhappiness I felt. He had showered me with so much unconditional love. His love and gratitude for me (he often stared into my eyes full of love) made me realize that he is my source of strength. When I felt thankful and good about him, I felt as if I was liberating the pain I felt; I was at peace with his death. If my zack is alive, he would want to see me happier and grounded rather than in a sober state. This incident clearly points out the underlying principle of coherence. When I want a relationship to be healthier, I must see the other person as a source of strength rather than weakness. And to accomplish that, we need to reflect on positive emotions.

For this purpose, you need to understand how to train your mind and handle yourself first. For only then can you extend your love to your child. The following section is all about how to train your mind, which is the key factor in deciding your happiness.

Training Your Mind – the Key Factor for Happiness

You can never control your mind. You can only train your mind. Thoughts run in your mind continuously like a stream of river. These thoughts are predominantly from your subconscious and tend to pop up automatically. You can never stop them but only manage them. Why? It is an automatic process, so you are unaware of the thoughts running in the back of your mind. 90 percent of your thoughts are replayed from your subconscious. Your subconscious mind documents all your past experiences, good and bad, without any differentiation. Your subconscious mind is a repository of data that contains all your painful and pleasant memories from the moment you were born till now.

Your mind is like a chatterbox that keeps generating thoughts without your conscious effort. When you use your intellect, a higher facility of the conscious mind, you can notice the quality of your thoughts at a given moment. Why do you need to notice your thoughts? Each thought will generate a corresponding feeling. If you think positively, "I can do this. It is possible!" subsequently, you will feel good. But if you think, "I cannot do this, or this is tough," you will feel inadequate or unhappy. These feelings will directly affect your actions and behavior. Thus your feelings decide what you do in a given situation. If you feel tired or sad, you will have trouble playing or interacting with your children happily. It is essential to feel good to keep your actions positive or useful.

As a mom, you will worry when your child misbehaves, or something bad happens to them. This may not be the right thing to do. If you allow the outside situation to control your thoughts, you may feel like a victim. You may wonder how to remain undisturbed when something unfavourable happens. It is possible if your mind is trained to stay in the present moment. According to Eckhart Tolle, the renowned author of "The Power of Now", there is no past or future; everything is present. Your brain, the physical organ of the mind, knows only the present moment and reacts to the triggers outside. When you recall any bitter, past memory stored in your brain, you tend to relive the negative feelings associated with that memory. The brain doesn't differentiate between past, present, and future as it functions from the current reality. So, the brain automatically releases stress chemicals cortisol and adrenaline, which cause you to feel the same emotion again. The emotions associated with that particular painful memory will be trapped in each cell of your body. These emotions were unprocessed, which means that when the incident happened, your emotions were suppressed. If you repeatedly replay the old memory, the same emotion will start vibrating at a particular frequency. This will cause you to draw more of that emotion (harmful) and create a mental blockage. Slowly they are felt as pain in your body. For example, if your child got hurt in a fight with the sibling and cries, as a parent, you have to allow them to process the emotion fully at that moment without any hindrance. If you shout or condemn the act and stop the child's crying, the suppressed emotions will be trapped in your child's body. This will make them more vulnerable to inflammation and cause diseases in the body.

The constant secretion of stress hormones in the body will put your mind in survival mode. Your brain will be threatened, not because of the real danger, but due to your imaginary fear of the future or continued dwelling in the painful past. Stress is nothing but a continuous focus on the next moment. You are drawn into the future, which never exists except in your mind. This excessive focus on the imaginary future will lose your connection with the present moment.

By training your mind, it is possible to keep it grounded in the present moment. In the present state, your mind doesn't perceive any real danger. When your mind is present, you always have a choice of what to think, feel, and do. Now you start taking faith-based action instead of indulging in fear-based action.

In 2008, my son was studying tenth class; I was worried he would have trouble passing his public exams. I was in a state of constant worry (in fact, I was not even aware that I was worried). This constant worry became fear which then turned into anxiety. My mind kept telling me, "What if something bad happens and he fails? What if he loses one year of his life?" I lost control of my conscious mind and started feeling anxiety in my body every morning. He would often skip school due to his anxiety about facing exams. So, every morning I would be anxiously working in my kitchen, peeping into his room now and then to check if he had woken up for school. This ritual continued till his college days. One fine day, I realized how I subjected myself to stress under the assumption that if my son failed his exams, he would lose one year, and therefore I would fail as a mom. Instead of focusing on my fear-based thoughts, I spent my time trying to control my son's behavior. As a mom, I was rather preoccupied with my fear of failing as a mom, rather than helping my son who was anxious about his exams. This happened because I lost touch with my consciousness and gave my subconscious mind free reign. If I had been more mindful, I could have handled the situation better and helped my son find a way out of his misery.

When a thought crosses your mind, you can either give it attention or ignore it altogether. When you provide it with attention, you are feeding energy to it. Gradually, you start identifying with it.

Subsequently, a neural pathway is etched in your brain. Hence, always be mindful of your thoughts, or you will be left at the mercy of your mind. If you are in the present moment, you will be conscious and aware of your actions. If you look closely, you will notice that fear and faith are invisible forces of energy that determine your actions. While fear-based energy will prevent you from taking any useful actions, faith-based energy will motivate you to take the right action.

The next section is about the deciding factor behind your happiness. The need to be in control or the fear of losing control is the primary reason for the parental stress you face in your life. Once you know the reality of who controls your life and what is under your control, you can get rid of stress effortlessly.

Who Controls Your Life: You or Your Mind?

Before we delve deeper to understand who is in charge of your life, let me shed some light on essential universal laws that govern your life. 12 universal laws form the basis of everything from the tiniest electron to the largest Sun. We are all governed by these laws, and our brains and minds are no exception. A person unaware of these universal laws will also be influenced by them. Let me give you an analogy. When you violate a rule in aforeign country, you will still have to face the consequences irrespective of the fact that you were unaware of the rule. The gravitational force will work no matter who you are. Thus learning and understanding the most important universal laws will help you live a more purposeful life.

Novalee wilder, a numerologist and author who works with the laws of the universe, mentions the most important law as the "Law of Divine Oneness." This law states that "We are all connected through creation; every single atom inside of you is connected in some way, shape, or form to the rest of the universe you move through." This explains how as a mom, you feel more in tune with your child, and experience an oneness with your child. The moment your child suffers or undergoes any hardships, you will be the first person to feel upset or worried.

Just learning the laws of the universe will not make a difference in your life. Applying these laws in your day-to-day activities will make a huge difference to your state of happiness. The universal cosmic energy flows towards you and through you. This pure, powerful cosmic energy has no boundaries or direction. When it is flowing through your consciousness, your thoughts will power them up and give them a sense of direction. Unfortunately, most of the time, you would be operating in autopilot mode, not conscious of what you are thinking or feeling inside. Autopilot mode involves your habitual thinking, feeling, and behavior stored in your subconscious mind. In autopilot mode, you carry out most activities that involve no thinking at all, like brushing, driving, dressing, cooking, and more. Your body can perform these activities without the presence of your conscious mind. Moreover, autopilot mode means you will be living in the past, influenced by repetitive thinking patterns and emotions. Only with awareness can you create new thoughts and feel new emotions.

Based on quantum science, your energy flows where your attention goes. If your attention is always on things that don't go as planned, you will vibrate at that frequency. Here, vibration refers to your feelings. Every feeling will be vibrating at a particular frequency, and based on the law of vibration, if you feel low you will be vibrating at a lower frequency. Similarly, if you feel good or elevated, you will vibrate at a higher frequency. The law of vibration states that "Everything in the universe has a frequency and a vibration," "Nothing ever stands still; everything is moving". It is also said that even after you die, your body cells keep moving when observed under the microscope. The law of vibration is more important than the law of attraction. The law of attraction is the ability to attract whatever you focus on into your lives.

Everything around us is energy. Space, air, water, light, plants, animals, stones, and even human beings are forms of energy. The presence of consciousness is what makes a difference. When you consciously think of a desire, you are vibrating at a higher frequency, which means that what you want will be available in the quantum field (higher frequency). You need to match your vibration to that higher frequency to get what you want. You will naturally attract what you want when you are in harmony with it. This means that you need to take care of your vibration, which is nothing but how you feel at any particular moment. This way, you will be accountable for your feelings and actions, preventing any chance of merely reacting. So, whenever you face a hurdle in your life, instead of blaming your children or anyone, you focus on your own feelings (vibrations).

The law of attraction is simple enough to understand. Nearly all scriptures explain them clearly. You ask for it, it is given, and you receive. When you are very clear about what you want, and you desire it from your heart, it is created in the parallel realm of the quantum field. Now the only question is, are you matching the frequency of that desire vibrating at a higher frequency. It is similar to ordering something on Amazon but not being present to collect it from the delivery person (if you are not present, it is not delivered to you). Your logical mind, the mind that is always in doubt, will never allow you to achieve what you want. Only when you allow yourself to increase your vibration and feel good, instead of feeling low, sad, angry, or bitter, will you match the vibration of your desire. To achieve this, you need a higher level of consciousness. Your current level of consciousness will not be enough to attain what you want. This is where we realize the need to partner with a higher source of infinite intelligence. Do you want to feel this power? Notice your breath and ask yourself who is regulating your breath when you are too busy to even think about it.

Now a question arises, what prevents you from maintaining your vibration at a higher level? As mentioned in the earlier section, it is the barrier called your mental programs wired in your subconscious mind. Mental programs are nothing but conditioned thought patterns or beliefs that control most of your habitual behaviour. You may think you are conscious and aware of what you think, say, and do. Sadly, most of you are operating in autopilot mode, giving your subconscious mind free reign. You know that your subconscious mind is programmed from outside, and you do not train this vast space. How can you take full control of your life if that is the case? You are never conscious of all dimensions or factors that decide the outcome of any situation. As your conscious mind occupies only 5 percent of your brain, you are at the mercy of the subconscious mind, which takes up almost 95 percent of your brain. The challenge is staying in the focus mode and being mindful of every moment. If you are not in control, your reptilian complex, a part of your subconscious mind will decide to do one of these three things before your conscious mind decides upon a plausible action.

1. If familiar and safe, your brain proceeds with action.
2. If familiar and unsafe, your brain avoids the action.
3. If completely unknown, your brain will stop and wait for more information.

In fact, it may seem as though you don't have any free will. To be honest, it is partially true, but you always have free will to deny it. Benjamin Libet, recipient of the Virtual Nobel Prize in Psychology for his pioneering achievements in the experimental investigation of consciousness, initiation of action, and free will, has proved scientifically that a decision is made in your brain up to. 02 to. 07 seconds before you become aware of it. This doesn't mean that you are just a passive observer, and you don't have any control over your life. Depending upon the familiarity and safety of the stimuli outside, your mind chooses from one of the three actions. The moment something happens outside (the stimuli), the brain will try matching the stimuli with the past data in your subconscious mind. If the stimulus is familiar and non-threatening, the brain will bring up the corresponding neural pattern, which will be filled with appreciative, loving, and satisfying thoughts. Similarly, if the stimulus is familiar, but the brain feels threatened, it will trigger a neural pattern that is full of discouraging and fearful thoughts. You will start to release stress hormones cortisol and adrenaline into your bloodstream. If you stay in the same stressful environment with a similar stimulation, your body will suffer the setbacks of the stress.

Your choice will vary according to the mental programs in the subconscious mind. So, there will be a default neural pattern that will stay out of your control. Though it looks like you don't have control, you can rewire and override the default pattern that occurs repeatedly by being mindful and aware.

When I was in college, my English lecturer asked me to complete a report writing assignment. Even today, I vividly remember begging my cousin, who was barely a year older than me, to write the article. She was annoyed with me as I did not even attempt to write a few words. Most teachers told me that writing is not my strong suit when I was a student. My mom and dad also reinforced that belief often. The thought "I am not good at writing" unknowingly went into my subconscious mind and got programmed by repetition. I didn't use my intellect to question or discriminate the thought but merely allowed it to sink into my subconscious mind. Each thought, when repeated, becomes a belief. This belief served as a barrier while I was writing this book too. I started to experience writer's block, a common problem many writers face. This limiting belief was one of my mental programs. Thanks to the

neuroplasticity of the brain, I was able to overcome it. So each time I realized this imprinted thought was popping up, I managed to stop writing using my awareness. While I had trouble stopping the speed at which the negative emotional pattern arose in my body, with consistent effort, I was able to overcome the temptation. My new behavior subsequently modified my neural pathway, thanks to the brain's neuroplasticity.

Hence it is very imperative to modify or reprogram your subconscious mind as and when required. To modify your mental programs, first, you need to know your limiting beliefs or emotions stored in the subconscious mind. You may not be aware of it if your focus is mostly on external factors. So the first step in taking charge of your life is identifying the mental programs in your subconscious mind. Is it possible to control all your impulses, desires, instincts, and innate drives that arise from your subconscious mind? Maybe not, but with awareness, you can rewire the old patterns and move towards what you want. The reason for failure in life or relationships is the inability to be in control over yourself. You end up feeling helpless, frustrated, angry, or sad. In stressful situations, you may blame yourself or others, depending on your coping strategy.

Based on the quantum field of science, I would help you understand, how to create your own reality by reprogramming your subconscious mind in stressful situations.

In quantum physics, it is understood that your reality is created with attention. Your attention turns the subatomic particles into everything you have in your life. This is based on the Heisenberg principle. In a famous experiment, the scientist found that when a person observes the electron through a slit, the subatomic particle electron behaves either as a wave or a particle. So in a given moment, an electron can be partially a wave and a particle.

I was fascinated by quantum field principles and tried to connect them to my understanding of relationship dynamics. We all know that we are made up of atoms and molecules. If we see our body tissues under a microscope, the cells are nothing but a cluster of atoms with protons, neutrons, and electrons closely vibrating together at a particular frequency. Ultimately, we are a collection of tiny particles with pure consciousness vibrating in this universe. Only an observer can make a difference in the behavior of the electron. Similarly, every individual can make a difference by observing themselves. In fact, you can also monitor the other person who is made up of atomic particles and interpret them as the kind of person you want them to be. The waveform is a field of unlimited possibilities, whereas the particle form is the reality. For example, if I come from a conscious state filled with love and compassion, I will notice similar goodness in others. The outcome will naturally be what I intend to see.

How you live now is based on these three things:

1. The limiting beliefs that you hold within
2. The self-talk that you subject yourself to
3. The self-image that you hold

These 3 things decide how and where your attention is focused and how frequently you live your day-to-day life.

Why do you find it challenging to sustain your frequency of happiness or have trouble going with the flow of life at ease? Because you are an evolving being, who is endowed with divine consciousness capable of creating your own reality. Animals, birds, and insects blend with nature to live peacefully. They don't fight or resist nature. The water flows and finds its pathways accordingly. The fire spreads its wings and expands to accommodate. The wind blows in the space it occupies. Nothing goes against the environment. Even a chameleon changes its colour to blend with its background. The only reason we humans resist or suffer is the disorientation we feel inside. Our conscious nature wants to expand to the true essence of what we are, but when environmental factors restrict us, we suffer. The higher faculties such as willpower, rational thinking, reasoning, imagination, intuitiveness, and memory help us create our own reality in this world. The paradox is that we are given a limited vehicle called the body to do things or act through this higher intelligence. Earlier, humans associated themselves more with the body than their higher intelligence. But, in recent years, humans have realized the power of intellect, the mind, and its struggles. This is where we start to go against with reality of our environment by fighting, running away, or just freezing. Humans have developed different coping strategies since the primitive stages of life. We find this continues even in this era of information, where people feel powerful or victimized in situations. One who rises beyond the case by utilizing their higher faculties is the person who thrives in the environment successfully.

When you think about something quite often, you create an image in your mind. This image is made based on the past experiences stored in your mind or images that were collected from current ongoing experiences. Images are the only way the subconscious understands your wants or desires. When you get emotionally involved, the image gets charged. The image becomes the vehicle that transports you to reality through your nervous system. In the earlier chapters, we saw that feelings are the subconscious language. Images fused with emotions are more potent than just thoughts with images. And so, by aligning your conscious and subconscious minds, you can induce motivation. That is mainly why merely thinking positive reviews does not make you a positive person. You need to dig deeper within yourselves and start believing you are the happy mom to become one.

To understand this concept better, let's try and understand the neuroscience of creating your own reality.

When you can make your belief match your mind's desire, you become one. You need to clearly understand what it will look like and how you feel about it in your mind. Once your mind knows what you want (even what you don't wish to), your brain will initiate RAS (Reticular Activating System). RAS is a bundle of nerves at our brain stem that filters out unnecessary information, ensuring that your attention is only spent on things that matter. Same way, it will look for information that validates your beliefs. RAS is the entryway to your conscious awareness. It acts like a switch that helps you swap from autopilot mode to focus mode. For example, if you want your child to be kind and cooperative, you need to picture your child with a smiling face speaking kindly to you. Instead, if you imagine your child's cranky and yelling image in your mind, it will become a reality. That is one of the major reasons why you need to stop complaining about or criticizing your child's behavior.

It does not matter whether your beliefs are good or bad, as the universal intelligence that is flowing through you is immortal. It doesn't care what you plan; it just gives back what you sow. It is similar to whatever you plant on fertile ground; whether it is a thorny plant or a sweet mango side by side, both grow into individual trees. In this instance, the fertile ground is your subconscious mind. Whatever you sow into it sprouts according to the supportive environment. Here, the supportive environment refers to the emotional vibes surrounding your thoughts.

You need to recondition your body and rewire your mind. I urge you not to wait until a considerable trauma or crisis hits to change your habitual thinking pattern. Rather than waiting for a state of suffering, start to learn and change from a state of happiness and inspiration? I will guide you through a process in the 5th chapter to help you rewire your old habitual beliefs. By creating new beliefs, you will feel good about yourself.

The next chapter is about parenting, and we will discuss the factors that affect the child's personality and the significance of self-love.

POINTS TO PONDER:

1. You are living in two worlds simultaneously. One is the physical world you observe, and another is the non-physical quantum inner world within you.
2. If your mind wanders, you can neither focus on the present moment nor guide your children appropriately. As true happiness can be found only in the present moment.
3. Rather than operating in autopilot mode, choose your thoughts carefully so that they are aligned with the outcome you want. You can get the intended results only when your thoughts, emotions, and actions are coherently aligned.
4. Suffering denotes that your mind is not in the present moment or focussed mode. As a mom, you may have early imprints of bitter incidents that you often recall or suppress unconsciously. These dark shades of memories are the root cause of your sufferings.
5. The brain doesn't differentiate between past, present, and future as it functions from the current reality. So, whenever you recall any bitter, past memory stored in your brain, you tend to relive the negative feelings associated with that memory.
6. The higher faculties such as willpower, rational thinking, reasoning, imagination, intuitiveness, and memory help us create our own reality in this world.

* * *

Chapter III

Parenting Matters

Healthy Parenting

Factors that Impacts the Child's Personality

The Mother-Child Attachment Style

Self Love: Basic Ingredient for Being a Happy Mom

Quantum Science and Parenting

Chapter 3

Parenting Matters

Your children came through you and not from you.
And though they are with you yet they don't belong to you.
You can give them your love only and not your thoughts,
As they have their own thoughts.

– Khalil Jibran

Healthy Parenting

The primary aim of parenting is to raise the child as an adult who is emotionally, mentally, physically, and socially independent in society. All parents want their children to be ultimately happy and peaceful.

Healthy parenting is not a myth. It is an art of parenting that comes from being a mindful mom. To be conscious is not merely being in the present moment but also using your awareness and inner presence in whatever you do. This involves training your mind to focus on the outcome you want to achieve. Shifting from autopilot mode to the focused mode is essential when you are with children. The child tends to use you as the emotional GPS until the age of 7, as their conscious mind is not fully developed. Until the age of 18yrs, they may depend on you for guidance and emotional support until they become emotionally independent. After they grow into adults, you need to be present only when they reach out to you for support. This is healthy parenting.

Healthy parenting is similar to a designer customizing a dress for his/her clients. One size doesn't fit all. Equity is more important than equality. Every child has different emotional needs. One child will expect more attention from you than your other child. If you have a mental program, "I am not important, " you may approach your child from that belief in your subconscious mind.

We all know that bananas are perfect for health. But can all kinds of people eat it regularly? The answer is no. People with diabetes can eat it in moderation only, and a person with kidney issues needs to avoid it altogether. Similarly, good parenting skills are not universal for all children. What I mean by healthy parenting here is the one that works out for you and your child. Good parenting is all about what works out for most children, which involves being firm and kind. The essence of healthy parenting is when your child feels accepted and approved by you. This will subsequently lead to self-approval and self-acceptance. Parents need to assure that they accept the child without any strings attached. This may seem unrealistic as parents are products of conditional acceptance. On what grounds can we expect children to be accepted or approved by their parents? Every mom needs to make her children feel **"Okay" and "Loved".** These are the two essential criteria for healthy parenting.

When I was a child, I never felt loved by my mom. It is not that she didn't shower her love on me or take care of me; it is my predisposition to focus mostly on her unwanted actions to reinforce my belief that "I am unlovable." My mom found it easier to show her love to my brother and younger sister as they were more receptive in nature. I had much difficulty receiving love and care from my mom as I was preoccupied with my own unwanted feelings. Till the age of 30 years, I conceded "I am unloved" due to my lack of awareness.

I was biologically programmed to be a rebel. I mean that I was a child who never gave up quickly. I tend to fight with my parents

and end up losing miserably. My sister, who is just one year younger than me, was passive, but she was smart enough to get what she wanted through my dad without fighting. My mom treated us both the same way. She always demanded obedience from us. My mom found it rather challenging to handle me as I did not submit to her authority. I got punished by her, while my sister escaped by keeping her head down. Once I went to a movie with my high school friends without informing my parents. I told a lie and went to the cinema. She came to know this, and I was caught red-handed as I hid under the bed, fearing her wrath. I often acted out as I felt controlled by my parents and wanted to rebel against their authority over me. If only my mom had modified her parenting style and given us some quality attention and priority, I would have been a different person. Maybe, her parenting style was apt for my sister as she was more cooperative and did not rebel against authority openly.

Factors that Impacts the Child's Personality

The predominant factor that determines your child's life is parenting. Other significant factors are genetic code, parents' personality, family structure, and school environment. The perception of the child and their predispositions play a significant role in shaping their personality. When a child is raised in a similar structural context as their parents, we cannot expect them to perceive things differently. Considering the collective consciousness paradigm, it is evident that most of today's parents are by-products of their own parents, who were also labeled "I am not OK". This brings to an important question, how do we break this curse from being passed on like hot potatoes from generation to generation?

If the parenting of previous generation parents had been perfect, then by default, we can expect a younger generation with a resourceful and healthier mindset. Unhealthy parenting and an unstable environment left the younger generation in tatters. A child's life is determined by multi-contextual factors and not the parenting style alone. I want to reiterate this firmly, as my life is a living example. If my parents were fully responsible for who I am today, I will give them all the credit. Only a skilled doctor could educate a student to become a doctor, or a skilled lawyer could train his junior to become a good lawyer. Similarly, a tree can bear fruits of its own origin only. If physical traits are passed on genetically, so can the mental traits. It is complicated to distinguish the propensity of parents to be responsible for their child's personality. A child's biological predisposition, often in the form of temperament, lays the foundation for their personality development. Recent research (NIMH, 2020) clearly indicates the impact of the enduring nature of early temperament on adult outcomes.

Let us dig into this deeper and see how each factor influences your child's personality.

Genetic or Epigenetic

Until now, there has always been a very long-standing question in the field of psychology. Is it nature (Gene) or nurture (Environment) that decides the personality of the child? Going by the previous stand, the genetic influence was the most predominant, accounting for more than 50 percent of a child's personality. I had always been very sceptical about this ratio. DNA is the perfect hereditary molecule, and the central dogma earlier was DNA rules your life, and you don't have any control over it. Genes cannot switch themselves on or off. In scientific terms, genes are not self-emergent. Something in the environment has to trigger your gene's activity.

One of my favourite scientists, Bruce Lipton, has done an extensive research to reveal the dynamics of genetics in our life. As a molecular biologist, he proved how the environment regulates gene activity. The science of genetics has proved that there are two ways of passing on hereditary information, one by nature (Gene) and another by nurture (Epigenetic). According to epigenetic research, the environment controls the gene's activity without modifying the genetic code. Your environment, and specifically your perception of the environment, changes your genetic activity.

According to epigenetics, your beliefs and your internal state governs the expression of the genes. The way you perceive things has an influence on your internal state of being. Your internal state includes your thoughts, beliefs you hold, the emotional state you choose to feel, and your self-talk. These aspects create changes at the cellular level. If your brain often perceives a threat, it will lead to the release of stress chemicals, which will affect blood constituents and subsequently modify your genetic expression. So, if you can modify the environment or your perception of the environment, you are in a position to shift from a victim state to a mastery state. Perhaps this will help you realize the massive responsibility you have in taking care of your emotional well-being.

Let's say you have two children having the same gene Y; the gene cannot be changed as it is the blueprint that you are born with. The blueprint by itself is not modified; you need a reader to interpret it and express it. Similarly, the Y gene expression constitutes the way of your life, your behaviour, and your character. The Y gene will remain unchanged. However, the way your children interact with their environment and how they choose to express themselves will decide how Gene Y evolves. He also mentions clearly that defective genes acting alone account for about 2 percent of our total disease load, the onset of disease, and a shortened life span. In contrast, exercise, good nutrition, a positive outlook on life, living in happiness and gratitude, giving back to the community, and experiencing love, especially self-love, all promote long and healthy life.

You know very well that 95 percent of your behaviour in a day is influenced by the invisible programming in your subconscious mind. Each and every minute, your child observes you while they grow up. A simple gesture of how often you smile can make a big difference in your child, based on how they perceive it. This is why it is so essential to be conscious of how you speak to them and treat them. The way you treat your child determines the type of environment they grow in. A positive, conducive environment and the child's perception of the environment decide the gene's expression.

Family Structure

One of the most influential factors on your child's personality is family. Thanks to my family roots for making me the person I am today. A healthy family represents the foundation of who you become in life. Building resilient families is a self-preservation approach for any rational and sane society. Only a progressive society will support all of its members in reaching their full potential as human beings. A research report (Family Paediatrics) showed that families are the most important influence in a child's life regardless of income, values, composition, and education (2003).

Both dad and mom need to develop a loving connection and bond with the child during the formative years. The first 7 years of a child's life are very crucial in determining its personality. Family structure plays an important role during these 7 years of the child. Parents who devote quality time to their children create a secure bond with their children, and so the child develops a strong attachment. The kind of environment that the child grows in decides the kind of relationship they have with their parents. An enriching and encouraging home environment can promote healthy growth and brain development which is filled with love, emotional support, and opportunities for learning and exploration.

If your living environment is restricted, noisy, and filled with hostility, your child's personality will be affected. If you are living in a joint family or a nuclear family where both parents work full time, the attention towards the child is divided. The child may seek out alternative forms of attention, which can lead to an emotional distance between the child and you. Similarly, unfriendly surroundings often cause children to freeze or hide negativity, making them more introverted.

There is no parenting manual to give you a perfect set of indicators for your child, but the best thing you can do is ensure that you are emotionally present for your child whenever they need it. You should also focus on keeping your household environment peaceful and joyful. The greatest environment for this is a calm and loving home that allows your child to improve his/her abilities. The absence of such a stimulating environment can have a negative impact on your child's personality development. As a mom, you can create opportunities for your child to discover their interests and instill a sense of curiosity within them so that they question everything and find solutions by themselves. As a mother, it is your obligation to expose your child to the right environment as it has a direct impression on their behavior, learning, and personality.

My uncle enrolled in a convent school near my place when I was 5 yrs old. As we lived in a joint family, my mother was dependent on my uncle's decisions for everything. Though I had some happy memories in school, I had a few unpleasant experiences which made me feel very inferior to myself. Due to constant comparison with my cousins, I developed an inferior feeling quickly. Once in my 10th standard, my teacher called out to me and asked me to read the English textbook. I was quite nervous, and as a result, I switched to my autopilot mode. The mental program "I am not good enough" got activated, and I started to fumble. I could neither find the

right pronunciation nor read it correctly. I felt so embarrassed and bad when my friends started to giggle at my performance. When I recollect this memory now, I don't feel the same emotions as I have rewired my brain. What I mean is that I have used my awareness to understand that just because I had trouble reading doesn't mean that I am not good enough. Moreover, I took measures to improve my vocabulary later in my thirties. I used to refer to a dictionary and learn three new words each day. This helped me speak well with confidence. I cannot blame my mom or dad for this class experience, as they could never have anticipated such an incident. Now I'm aware that it is my responsibility to understand and manage my emotions. It is so evident that how parents perceive their child has an immense impact on their life.

Family is the foundation for all your values, including your happiness, respect, acceptance, love, and success. I firmly believe that family has to be a key pillar in a person's life if they want to live happy and meaningful relationships. Family forms the springboard for the community feeling or sense of belongingness in your child, which is essential for a healthy mindset. Family structure not only plays an important role in shaping children's health early in life, but it also creates the foundation for an adult's personal, educational, and economic success.

Parenting Style

Parenting is more significant in a child's life than the parent itself. Your actions and the way a child feels in consequence of your attitude towards them decide your parenting style. You may adopt a parenting style based on the experience you had with your parents. Parenting style refers to the type of emotional climate you provide for the child while you are rearing them. Feeling good is the essence of good parenting.

Emotional dependency is a very crucial factor in parenting. It is a well-known fact that a child's self-image is formed in their formative years, based on how he/she is treated and groomed by their primary caretaker. Most moms take the whole responsibility to nurture and raise the child in the initial stages through the child is emotionally dependent on both parents. It is the child who decides who her primary caretaker is and then creates an attachment to one parent.

Moms play a very significant role in each child's life, as they need to help the child feel loved and wanted. Research has extensively proved that the more you shower a child with affection, kindness, and unconditional positive regard in the early stage, the happier your child tends to be in the later parts of life. Whether it is unpleasant or pleasant, it goes directly to your child's subconscious as they don't use their conscious brain in the formative years. Without a mental filter, the child often feels helpless as they have little to no control over their mind and body. But things will change as they enter adolescence; because that is when their prefrontal cortex is developed, and they start filtering unwanted information from entering their subconscious mind.

All parents want to see their children happy and well-behaved as they grow up. Though intentions are good most of the time, they may not treat the child with respect and compassion. Instead, they may end up intimidating, threatening, or even pampering them, ruled by their fear. When can we say a parent is not parenting the child right? A simple way to understand this is by understanding the different parenting styles that parents exhibit. Although parents start with one parenting style, some of them end up with a different parenting style based on the child's temperament. Before explaining the five different styles of parenting, let me share an example that would give you more clarity on the concept of parenting.

I would like to share one of my experiences as a teen. Back then, half-saree was the commonly worn attire by teen girls. It was a traditional custom that after attaining puberty, girls who are now considered to be mature must stick to that attire. Though I refused it as much as I could, I was forced to wear it no matter how uncomfortable it was for me. In my eighth standard, my dad insisted that I wear it. It was a traumatic experience for me at that age as I was caught between keeping up my comfort and satisfying my parents. In one instance, I ran into the bathroom to escape them, but my dad threw water into the bathroom through the top window and made me come out. The action they took could be easily justified by saying that if I had obeyed their wish and worn the attire, things would have been much easier. I'm not here to argue about who is right or wrong. My argument is all about what is right. If we judge our actions, both of us would be wrong. My parent's behavior was threatening to me. Similarly, my rebellious behavior was not helpful in any way. I had a power struggle with my parents. Although I was poorly expressive, my strongly-determined attitude made up for it. The type of parenting that my mom used was authoritarian, which involved a lot of strictness and less emotional connection.

Now that the storytime is over let us discuss the five different styles of parenting. Take a closer look at each one and identify your parenting style.

The first one is the balanced style. It is considered optimal because there is a balance of separateness versus togetherness and stability versus flexibility. Balanced style parenting is moderate to high on both closeness and flexibility. The balanced parenting style is characterized by warm and nurturing parents who are emotionally supportive and responsive to their child's needs, encourage independence (with monitoring), are consistent and fair in dishing out discipline, and expect age-appropriate behavior.

The second one is the uninvolved parenting style. It is very low in closeness between parents and the child but is very high in flexibility. The uninvolved parenting style is characterized by low emotional connection, low responsiveness from parents to the child, high independence of the child from the parent (parents are disconnected from the child's life), highly negotiable rules that are loosely enforced, and a very few demands made on the child.

The third one is the permissive parenting style. It is very high in closeness between parents and child and also has very high flexibility. The permissive parenting style is characterized by parents who are overly protective of their child, very responsive to their child's every need, more of a friend to their child, lenient in discipline, and unlikely to make demands of their child.

The fourth is a strict or authoritarian parenting style. It is very low in closeness between parents and child and also has very low flexibility. The strict parenting style is characterized by strictly enforced rules, highly restricted child freedom, firm discipline, low responsiveness to child, and low emotional connection between parent and child.

The final one is the overbearing parenting style. It is very high in closeness between parents and child and also has high flexibility. The overbearing parenting style is characterized by overly-protective parents who cater to the child's every need and act more like a friend to the child while at the same time strictly enforcing a proliferation of rules with firm discipline.

Though the personality is determined by emotional traits passed on by parents, there are other multiple factors that impact or influence the child's growth into a responsible and happy adult. As each and every parent wants their child to be a forever happy individual who grows successful and achieves a good position within society and is deemed as a good human being, it is crucial to pick a parenting style that suits your child's needs.

Mother's Attitude Matters

Author Verny writes in her "Pre-Parenting: Nurturing Your Child" book that unborn children are constantly tuned in to their mother's every action, thought, and feeling. From the moment of conception, the experience in the womb shapes their brain and lays the groundwork for personality, emotional temperament, and the power of higher thought. This doesn't mean that only mom's attitude is responsible for the fetus' emotional well-being. Indirectly, the spouse's attitude, support, socio-economic status, mental freedom, and other sociological factors have a subsequent effect on your child's mental well-being.

As a mom, an attitude of being sensitized to a child's emotional needs, being mindful, and feeling resourceful will be a healthier one. Only by being in the present moment, in awareness, will you have the choice to choose how to respond than outright react. Your reactions have a great impact on the child, especially in their formative years from 0 to 7. The child's subconscious mind is open with no filter (Conscious mind) to discriminate or reason your actions. They are very sensitive to your facial expressions and changes in your body language. Facial expressions constitute 60 percent of your body language in communication. Your child's first language is body language which is a non-verbal communication tool. Your facial expression, voice tone, and body posture are more important than your verbal communication and the words you speak. Words constitute only about 6 to 8 percent of your communication with the children. The way you react leaves a huge impact on your child's behavior.

There are two most important questions a parent needs to ask before reacting to the child to keep your action coherent with intention. Is my action helpful for my child to become independent, and does it encourage them to use their inner guidance system? Is my action serving my child to become a happy individual? You may feel stressed not because of the child's misbehavior or routine chores pertaining to the child but mostly because of the unattainable expectations you have set out for yourself. There is a cognitive gap, a misplaced evaluation of your own self-image and the ideal self. As you experience this cognitive gap between who you are and what you would want to give rise to frustrations and irritations. This will make you blame others for not providing physical and emotional support at crucial times. The truth is the beliefs you hold about yourself are not supporting the goal that you want to accomplish. If you want to feel like a competent mom, you should have a supporting belief, "I am confident" and "I am efficient." These beliefs will induce encouraging thoughts such as, "I can complete this task on time." It is evident that your beliefs have an impending impact on your attitude and, more importantly, how your behavior and attitude program the lives of your children.

Every child is unique in their own way. As a parent, you hold beliefs that could make you feel unworthy and not good enough. Your beliefs determine how you treat your child and not what your child does. If you believe that your child needs to respect me, naturally, you may get hurt the moment your son or daughter speaks to you in an unfavorable way. That doesn't mean that you just walk away from them when they behave in a way that you dislike. What is important at that moment is how you treat yourself inside. The first step is to understand and accept that your children have their own choice of what they value or prefer in this world. Their values and your values will be different, and the same applies to your belief system. Your children behave the way they do because of what they believe and not what is good for parents.

I was living in a very big family, where my dad and his elder brother's family lived together. My mom was very particular in being obedient to elders. She had inculcated that value from her parents. I happened to be a child who was just the opposite. I was very particular in not obeying what others said and often displayed a rebellious attitude. We usually go out every weekend to a movie and then visit a hotel to have our dinner. It was one of my favorite times. I will wait every Saturday to go to a movie and then to our favorite restaurant, Bilal in Mount Road. Once my mom asked me not to reveal anything to my aunt if she asked about our outing and what each of us ate for dinner in the restaurant. Being a people-pleasing person, I did the exact opposite and revealed all information to my aunt. My mom got very upset and started to shout at me for not obeying her orders. She was not in a position to understand that I have different choices or beliefs. She took it personally and felt disrespected and hurt. She was not in a position to express her disappointment and explain the reason for her behavior. I, as a child, was unable to comprehend anything and was focused on her behavior of hitting me on my head. Each time I behave indifferently, I get negative attention from her. Unfortunately, I didn't know at that moment that I was creating a neural pathway, that I was not ok, not loved enough, and not good enough for my mom. My sister, who was smart enough, will never disclose anything to my aunt. My aunt, for that reason, would always question me rather than my sister. I have had some nice moments with my aunt in my childhood days. So, I had no reason to hide anything from her.

My mom may have failed to understand the fact that my actions and words were a reflection of my personality and not who she is. She was hurt, not because of my actions, but the meaning that she gave to herself when I did not obey her words. These meanings arise from her belief, "My child should listen and obey what I say". She showered me with love when I behaved the way she wanted, or she was in a very happy state of mind. I always wanted that same love from her. I was not in a position to know that my mom cannot always be perfect and consistent in her actions. It took me ages to realize that only the divine infinite intelligence is 24/7 available within my heart to take care of me and love me consistently.

Why do we want someone to love us consistently and unconditionally? Only when the mom or dad shows unconditional love will the child start to believe or feel loved inside. It is not just love, but only when they feel accepted unconditionally would they feel worthy enough to live in this world. I had been denied this love, which really affected my existence. The epitome of this phenomenon was passing on this belief or value to my children. I unknowingly passed down the same pattern to my children, which affected them badly. It took me many years to change the pattern of my thoughts and my belief system.

School

School is one of the integral parts in moulding a child's personality as the child spends most of their time in a classroom. As a mother, you know very well about your child's capacity, and based on that, you need to choose a school that would suit your child's needs. Furthermore, it's important to keep yourself up-to-date with your child's school happenings, consult teachers regularly, and interact with your child's peers and their parents. These are some of the significant functions of a good, concerned parent.

The mother has to ensure the child is provided a simulated learning environment at home in addition to the school's learning environment as it has a positive impact on the child's mental development. This comprises developing adequate cognitive, linguistic, emotional, and motor skills.

Nutrition

Nutrition is vital for the physical and mental growth of a child. Children need to develop healthy eating habits and eat more balanced nutritious foods as it has an effect on their immune systems. The child's immune system operates as an adjunct to developing a healthy mind and body. As a mom, it's essential to feed your child with balanced, wholesome food that constitutes carbohydrates, protein, fats, fibre, and vitamins.

Parenting Alone Doesn't Decide Your Child's Personality

Yes, parenting matters. It is essential in the first 7 years of your child's life. Later in life, parenting matters only in challenging situations. Research clearly indicates that parents and the parenting technique they use have little to no effect on the evolution of a child's personality. As children grow up, they start mimicking one of their parents. It is mostly the parent they spend most of the time with, and they are easily influenced by them. It is well known that children often seek the approval and acceptance of their peers. The temperament they are born with, and their experiences decide who they become. Your parenting techniques are the mediating factor that serves as the crux of your child's future.

In my life, I spent most of the time with my mom, and so I was influenced by her more than by my dad. She was a very strong and determined person. At the same time, she was a person who had extreme thoughts and emotions. She had a tough time dealing with her own emotions whenever my behavior was taxing to handle. As I

grew into an adult, I watched her either feel helpless or downright depressed when things didn't go her own way. I also became an intrinsically sad person due to the mental program I had received from her. Later in my life, the sudden loss of my loving brother shook me completely and made me ask existential questions, which led me to find my life's purpose. Since then, there was no looking back in my life. Yes, I embarked on a self-exploratory journey to find my true self.

In earlier stages, it is quite natural for a child to depend physically and emotionally on parents. Your child will depend on you for their physical (hunger, thirst, and sleep) and emotional (warmth, safety, and love) needs. Eventually, they will outgrow their dependency on you as they develop their conscious mind to think independently and identify what is good and what is not. Unfortunately, most mothers don't let go of their need to protect and control their children due to their inability to let go of their attachment.This is the primary reason for most unhappy parent-child relationships in the family.

In the following section, you will learn about the attachment that children develop with one of their parents, different types of attachment styles, their impact on a child's personality,and how it determines your child's self-image.

The Mother-Child Attachment Style

Attachment style refers to the way you respond emotionally to a person as well as your behavior and interactions with them. During the early childhood days, you develop an attachment to your primary caretakers, and it tends to remain persistent. This attachment style has a profound effect not only on your emotional development but also on the health of all your other relationships. Your style of attachment was formed at the very beginning of your life, during your first two years. Once established, it is a style that stays with you and impacts how you participate in intimate relationships and even how you parent your children. Understanding your style of attachment is helpful because it offers you insight into how you felt. It also clarifies ways that you are emotionally limited as an adult and what you need to change to improve your close relationships, like the relationship with your children. Fundamentally, your present attachment with your spouse reflects the relationship you had with your primary caretaker (mom, dad, aunt, nanny, etc.) as a baby. There are four main adult attachment styles: secure, anxious, avoidant, and fearful-avoidant.

Secure attachment style refers to your capacity to form secure, loving relationships with others. A securely attached person can trust others and be trusted, loved, and get close to others with ease. You will not be afraid of intimacy, nor do you feel disturbed when your partner or child moves away. They don't feel panicked when their partners need time or space away from them. They can have a healthy relationship with others without becoming totally dependent.

Anxious attachment style is evident by a deep fear of rejection. Anxiously attached people tend to be insecure about their relationships. They often worry about their spouse leaving them and always yearn for validation. They seem to be desperate and needy to be loved and accepted by their partner. They feel as though the partner doesn›t care enough about them.

Avoidant attachment style is a form of insecure attachment style evident by a fear of intimacy. People with avoidant attachment styles tend to have difficulty getting closer. They don't trust others very easily. They feel suffocated when their partner gets close. They prefer to stay distant from their partners and are mostly emotionally uninvolved in their relationship. They prefer to be independent and rely on themselves.

Disorganized is a combination of both the above two. In this style, people yearn to be loved and want to avoid it at any cost. They are not interested in developing a close, romantic relationship.

Largely, research studies on early attachment specify that less than 50 percent of the adult population possess a secure attachment as a child while growing up. These are children whose parents were emotionally available, understanding, and responsive. A child that was securely attached to a caretaker later becomes an "autonomous adult." They will be able to convey their needs, provide and accept affection, and stay autonomous. Secure adults are more likely to successfully handle stress, stay emotionally healthy, and enjoy fulfilling relationships.

Based on research studies, it is found more than 40 percent of the population who had an insecure attachment and has now become a parent who is an "entangled" and "dismissive" adult. Children tend to develop insecure attachment when their parents are emotionally unavailable, insensitive, or unresponsive and give mixed and unpredictable messages. Some of them may even outright reject their responsibilities too. Entangled and dismissing adults often feel disconnected from intimacy and find it difficult to understand what they are feeling. They often have difficulty speaking about how they feel about their own parents or about past relationships.

Each child comes into this world with unmet emotional needs that are unique to the propensity of the individual. These deep-seated unmet emotional needs lay the foundation for the child to evolve into a personality, in addition to their genetic predisposition, parent's emotional well-being, style of parenting, and any life-changing incidents. Therefore it becomes imperative for the mother to be sensitized to these unmet emotional needs along with the physical needs of their child.

You Have a Responsibility to Work Towards Establishing a Secure Attachment With Your Children

A mother who is mentally and emotionally available for the child can be in a position to take ultimate care of the child right from the infant stage. The more the child is exposed to unpleasant conditions or traumatic incidents, the more unhealthy the child's personality tends to be. On the other hand, when they feel connected with the people around, they feel more secure and safe. The feeling of safety and security makes children confident and courageous. Initially, the child is physically and emotionally dependent on the mother for everything, but slowly they become independent in their adolescence. Only later in their adulthood do they realize the importance of being interdependent.

I had an insecure, anxious attachment with my mom. Hence, I was always desperate to be loved and accepted by my husband, just as I was attached to my mom. I was suffering for a long time, feeling insecure and unloved in my marital relationship. Every time he prioritizes his friends and stays out late, I felt sad and angry that he ignored and disrespected my feelings. Once I realized this, I had to take some steps to fulfill my emotional needs instead of depending on my husband to make me feel secure. My consistent efforts helped me to shift from victim to victor state. I started to fall in love with myself. I realized how I had abandoned a part of me, my insecure inner child. I had not loved her for what she was; instead had rules or conditions to accept and embrace her. It was not up to my mom or husband to give me love or approval and make my inner child feel secure. It was my duty to overcome insecurity by integrating my conscious and subconscious minds. It is not about being detached, but by feeling integrated and whole inside, I never felt the need to depend on my husband to feel valued.

It is important to know your attachment style and its implications on your temperament, emotional quotient, relationships, and parent-child dynamics. Please refer to the appendix to assess your attachment style using a simple psychometric tool.

Having a close, secure bonding relationship is important for the emotional well-being of the child. When I mention close bonding, it doesn't mean that you need to be with your child around the clock. Staying connected with your child is different from staying with the child. You feel your child is an extension of your own self. It is like a part of your own body, even though the child grows into an adult. This is one of the primary reasons why you become so attached to your children and feel oneness even later in your child's adulthood.

To feel safe and secure, you need to connect to something that is more powerful than you. Initially, the child will try to connect with you to fulfill their emotional needs. At this stage, they form an attachment with you. This attachment determines how safe they feel inside. If you are available to the child to meet their physical and emotional needs, they will definitely feel safe and secure. If you fail to meet their needs appropriately, then the child will feel deprived, unwanted, and abandoned.

When I was young, I wanted to play and spend time with my mom. My mom was mostly cooking in the kitchen, as she had to take care of a large, joint family. My family was so closely knit that I called my uncle "appa". My uncle and my dad were both very close and had high regard for each other. We were a 10-member family living in the same house with a single operating kitchen. My mom had the responsibility of not only cooking for all of us but also for the guests and relatives who visited our home regularly. I was not in a position to understand all this, as my rational mind was not quite developed. I made a decision that when I grew up, I would never be in the kitchen. My need to connect and to feel

unwanted made me believe that "I am a good mom only if I give full attention to my child," which is not factual. Holding factual or neutral beliefs is more important than holding assumptions. The belief that I had affected my parenting later in my life when my first child was born. I was completely living the role of mom full time that I had lost myself. I was attached to my daughter that I was taking full-time care of her, not from a resourceful state but from the victim state of not being good enough. My victimized self and unmet emotional needs emerged and influenced my parenting. I was trying to do what was best for my child, but I was not aware that I made her feel she was not good enough. What I did not realize is that I can only give what I feel inside. I realized this only after she became an adult. It was a struggle for her to rewire this ingrained belief "I am not good enough".

The above experience clearly points out that my mom was unavailable for me when I wanted the most. This made me feel that I was not worthy, and subsequently, I passed on the same feeling down to my daughter. This is called generational trauma.

The type of attachment that you have with your child decides your child's self-esteem. Self-esteem is essential for your child to live happily and successfully in this world. Only when you love and respect yourself and have a positive image can you influence the self-image of your child.

The next section is about nurturing your child's self-esteem by loving and accepting yourself first.

Self Love: Basic Ingredient for Being a Happy Mom

Every human being is wired to be a social being. It doesn't matter how much you love your child; it matters how much you love your own self. Self-love is the most important ingredient that decides the quality of your parenting. Unfortunately, most mothers lack self-love, which ultimately determines the dynamics of parenting.

Self-love is not about putting yourself up on a pedestal and taking on a holier-than-thou attitude. It is all about genuinely treating yourself with the same compassion you would want from a most cherished friend or partner. You will be kind to yourself, understanding, caring, empathic, encouraging, and supportive of your endeavors. You take care of your emotions and emotional needs in a way that empowers you. Genuine self-love is built by you, not others.

We have a tendency to see self-love as being "self-centered." If you don't genuinely love yourself, then you cannot genuinely love others. Using the term self-love to promote narcissism is bad. And if you approach relationships to get "what you need," that's not love either. Genuine self-love is healthy, and it's about compassion. It is the process of satisfying your own emotional needs so that you do not have to depend desperately on others to meet your needs. Self-love is treating yourself with kindness and appreciation. You may wonder how to differentiate false self-love from genuine self-love. Genuine self-love is based on compassion rather than out of fear and deep-seated insecurities. False self-love creates poor emotional boundaries, trying to receive love by investing too much in a relationship and expecting results unconsciously. Genuine self-love doesn't use others to build in any way, including the act of "giving" or "loving."

This is similar to our relationship with one of our physical needs, food. You know when to eat, how to eat, and when to stop eating. You distinguish your own needs, when it feels good and when it no longer does, and you respond accordingly.

Healthy interpersonal relationships are the same way. You don't have to go hungry or stuff yourself up. You don't expect others to feed you. You don't try to fill your stomach by feeding others. And you definitely don't force-feed anyone to cover up for starving yourself. Similarly, as a mom, you need to be responsible enough to satisfy your own emotional needs rather than expecting your child to fulfill them. Only when you are deprived of feeling loved and respected, do you start to label yourself as a good or bad mom.

This deprivation of self-love is the primary reason why most moms suffer. When you are not happy, how can you respond to your child positively? Every one of us has a rational part (thinking mind) and an emotional part (feeling mind) within us. Let us label the part that observes both these parts as "you" (the divine part or superconscious mind). When your child does something unacceptable, your emotional part, also known as your inner child, will immediately react. Whenever you react without awareness in your autopilot mode, you release stress hormones cortisol and adrenaline into your bloodstream. Imagine you are continuously in the same environment with the same stimulation, then your body will suffer the setbacks of stress.

Now the pertinent question is if you love yourself will you subject yourself to this suffering. You may now ask how I avoid my child who is living with me. You know that it is impossible to always withdraw or run away from the situation. Usually, most of you either fight with your children or avoid getting hurt by moving away or stopping the conversation midway. How you react depends on the previous emotional experiences you had with your child. If your emotional experiences were mostly happy and pleasant, your brain uses those pleasurable memories that are stored in your subconscious mind. In this context, your inner child will not abruptly react but send neutral or positive thoughts from the subconscious mind. This inner child is in a state of calmness as there is an absence of unpleasant memories. This might not be true if you had not shown consistency and stability earlier. The inner child will automatically react as it gets threatened. The only way to calm your inner child is by giving attention to it, either by questioning or encouraging. The other way is by actively ignoring it. You will not ignore it completely, but with awareness, you can address your inner child's feelings and take the right action. Problems arise only when you are unaware of the cry of your inner child, and it ends up pouring out its distress onto your child. Eventually, you need to either suppress or fight with the inner child. The inner child may get stronger day by day, as the power of the subconscious mind is more than your conscious mind.

Long ago, my inner-child was feeling very disrespected and shameful. This was due to the humiliation I endured in my childhood whenever my dad compared me with my cousins and told me, "You are not worthy of a penny." It did not make much sense when I was a kid, but later it had a huge impact on my sense of self-worth. Whenever I had an opportunity or wanted to do something out of my way, these thoughts would arise from my subconscious mind and make me feel unworthy. This was stopping me from moving forward and attracting opportunities in my career. The lack of self-love only made things worse. But, eventually, I reframed my thoughts and affirmed myself, "I am unique", "I am worthy", and "I love myself". Once I implanted this affirmation into my subconscious mind by consistent repetition, I was able to soothe my inner child.

When you start to realize that you are the only person who can love and embrace your inner child, you will take 100 percent responsibility for your actions. Then you will never blame yourself or your child, as you are aware that lack of self-discipline is the primary reason for everything that goes wrong in your relationship. When I realized this, I made an effort to practice mindfulness regularly.

Mindfulness is all about being in the present moment in attention, non-judgmentally with awareness. I prefer to call this state the quantum state. Let us take a closer look at this concept in the following section.

Quantum Science and Parenting

According to quantum mechanics, everything, including humans, are a wave form. You are a luminous body of energy that extends beyond your physical body and mind. Your internal energy is in a continuous communal process with the environmental energy field. If you could travel inside your body and go beyond the skin, the bones, the organs, the tissue, the cells, the blood, neurons, and the subatomic particles, and then beside the tiniest particle-quarks, you will observe a vacant space, the quantum field. Quantum is the energy field that is an extension of your physical body. Everything is energy. The energy exists in either particle (body) or wave (mind). Waves make everything possible. Particles are what you see in the real world. There is a third component which is nothing other than your own self, the pure consciousness. Ask yourself this: is your attention on the possibility (quantum field) or the limitation (reality) of the child?

A quantum mom is a happy mom. Understanding the concept of quantum is as important as unveiling your true self. Since my childhood, as a science student, I had a great curiosity to learn the science behind everything. When I learned about quantum science, I was fascinated by this double-slit experiment that proved the very existence of our true nature.

The famous two-slits experiment conducted by physicist Heisenberg focused on proving that energy is a wave. Physicists experimented earlier in 1920 and found that light exists as waves.

When they repeated the same experiment with electrons, expecting it to show particle behavior, they were exposed to pattern interference, i.e., the same outcome. So, they placed a detector to observe the electron's activity. To their surprise, they found that the electron displayed particle behavior on the screen rather than acting like a wave (the pattern interference). They found that when the electron was noticed by the detector, it showed particle behavior. The process of observation made all the difference in the w electron's behavior. Now the question is, "How did the electron know that someone was observing? What made the electron change itself to a particle? It has been documented that scientist Heisenberg had traveled to India and met Rabindranath Tagore to understand how the presence of consciousness made all the difference.

This concept intrigued me for a long time. Did you know that when each of us is put under a microscope, we will become atoms and molecules vibrating at a particular frequency? Thus, we all are bundles of energy. The presence of different levels of consciousness, the invisible life force that permeates our whole universe, makes a lot of difference. As an observer, when I (consciousness) notice or perceive the other person (electron), they transform into reality (particle). For example, if I see my child as capable and I feel it in my body, I am tuned into that frequency. Naturally, as an observer, I create the reality by just transmuting the non-physical quality of confidence into a physical reality.

This is the basic premise of being a happy mom, as your thoughts and feelings must be aligned with what you desire for your child. They grow up to become the person you want them, rather than a person you detest. Steven Stosny, a relationship therapist and an author, has noticeably mentioned this behavior principle in close relationships. Behavior follows focus and we're likely to get more of what we focus on. So, it's very important to focus on what you want from your child and not on things that you hate. If you constantly accuse and complain negatively about your child's behavior, you will attract more of it. This will create a distance in your relationship. If you are going to focus on them being cooperative and kind, you will get more of it, only by focusing on what you want (example: being kind), not on what you don't want (being harsh). In fact, I have found that the more we focus on the unwanted behavior of a child, the more we will be unclear about our own evaluation.

Recently, when I visited my daughter, we had a simple issue of misunderstanding, which left me feeling slightly disturbed. She was also feeling a bit irritated due to my carelessness. At that moment, my emotions made things murkier. As my focus was on my emotions, I was completely unable to empathize or connect with her. My focus was on her unhelpful (tone) behavior of hers rather than what actually happened. Later, when I realized this, I focused on what I wanted from her and not what I didn't want from her. And also, I shifted from the state of being a helpless mom to a confident mom. I repeated and affirmed within myself, "I am a confident and loving mom" every time I interacted with my daughter. That was a useful exercise that left me feeling clear and good. That created a huge shift in my self-image, and miraculously our relationship started to mend.

As a mom, you need to feel like an effective parent by fully understanding and appreciating your child's uniqueness. In the next chapter, we will explore the significance of a mom-child relationship, how to respond to and how to prevent reacting to your child, learning lessons from your children, avoiding the aspect of creating dreams for your child, and the key factor in a mom–child relationship, unconditional acceptance.

POINTS TO PONDER:

1. Healthy parenting is similar to a designer customizing a dress for his/her clients. One size doesn't fit all. Here, equity is more important than equality.
2. Every mom needs to make her children feel "Okay" and "Loved". These are the two essential criteria for healthy parenting.
3. Things that would mostly influence a child's personality are: epigenetic, family structure, parenting style, and mother's attitude.
4. Attachment style refers to the way you respond emotionally to a person as well as your behaviour and interactions with them. There are four main adult attachment styles: secure, anxious, avoidant, and fearful-avoidant.
5. Self-love is not about putting you, up on a pedestal and taking on a holier-than-thou attitude. It is all about genuinely treating yourself with the same compassion you would want from a most cherished friend or partner.
6. The basic premise of being a happy mom is that your thoughts and feelings must be aligned with what you desire for your child. So, they grow up to become the person you want them, rather than a person you dislike intensely.

* * *

Chapter IV

The Significance of a Mom-Child Relationship

Responding or Reacting – the Deciding Factor of Quality Relationships

Motherhood – Breaks or Makes You

Child is Your Guru: Learning Lessons from Your Children

Never Dream for Your Child, Dream for Yourself

Unconditional Acceptance – the Key to a Healthy Relationship

Chapter 4

The Significance of a Mom-Child Relationship

"Parents are the ultimate role models for children. Every word, every movement, and action affects. No other person or outside force has a greater influence on a child than a parent."

– Bob Keeshan

The relationship between a mother and her child is a unique bond that nurtures the whole growth and development of a child. It lays the groundwork for the child's behaviour, personality, traits, and values. According to various studies, it has been found that children who have a healthy relationship with their parents are more likely to develop positive relationships with other people around them. They can create secure bonds and friendships with their peers. They will be in a better position to regulate their emotions when confronted with stress and difficult situations.

Children who have a secure and positive relationship with their parents learn critical skills and values that ensure their future success. Moreover, a secure attachment with one parent helps promote a child's cognitive, emotional, and social development. It also helps them display positive social behaviors most of the time. The healthy involvement of parents in their children's day-to-day life helps ensure that their kids perform better socially and academically. The primary contextual factor that decides the child's healthy relationship is their mother's availability in crucial situations. A Turkish research study showed that the emotional availability of both parents was related to positive outcomes in mental health, emotional regulation, relationship success, and social support as children entered adulthood. The most significant indicators of a close and healthy relationship between parent and child is the amount of warmth, sensitivity, and responsiveness showered by parents on their child.

When your child (a teenager or a young adult) is undergoing a stressful situation, they get disturbed and feel disconnected from their inner guidance system. That moment your child expects you to be beside them, not for comfort but to connect with you and feel safe and secure. Your child is not looking for solutions or readymade answers, but they want you to validate their negative feelings. Your child will listen to you but will arrive at a decision on their own that will be uninfluenced by others. They will listen to you and cooperate with you only when they feel connected to you and trust you completely.

When your child fails to develop a positive identity at the age of 12 or 13, it could affect their personality. They tend to become either emotionally dependent or emotionally detached. And they will have trouble making their own decisions in stressful situations. They may be inclined to be doubtful about themselves and end up finding fault or blaming others for challenging situations in their own life. Most research findings suggest that socioeconomic status, parental mental well-being, and social environment are the most serious risks for behavioral problems and cognitive performance issues in the general child population. It was also found that parents with greater mental distress passed it onto their children in the form of emotional distress.

I remember how my mom was emotionally unavailable to me when I was growing up. When I say that I wanted my mom to be available, I mean that I wanted her to be there for me when I needed her presence the most. As this was the way, I felt loved deep within me. As we lived in a joint family, she found it very difficult to find time to spend with me. She spent most of her time in the kitchen rather than with me. I used to earn so much for my mom's presence. I yearned for her cuddles and wanted her to listen to my conversations. Sometimes, I felt very sad when I returned from school to find her absent at home (she would have gone to her mom's place). Irrespective of her temperament, she prepares yummy upma or dry fish gravy with rice when I get back from school. It is not the food that depicted how my mom truly loved me; it's the feelings that were imprinted as neural pathways in my brain. My brain had associated that memory with feeling loved.

Every child is born with specific unmet emotional needs that the parents are obliged to acknowledge and fulfill until their child becomes an adult. If the child has no physical or emotional needs, the parent will not develop any relationship. Hence, it's observed that the parents are responsible for satisfying the physical and emotional needs of their children till they become emotionally independent. When both parent and child are needy, a beautiful relationship will not exist.

To establish a happy mom and child(young adult) relationship, both of you need to feel self-sufficient and be respectful to each other. So you need to shift from,

"I need", "I expect", and "I want" to "***I am***".

Responding or Reacting – the Deciding Factor of Quality Relationships

In any relationship, two people interact verbally and non-verbally to communicate their thoughts and feelings to each other. Similarly, the child will communicate with their parents to express his/her physical and emotional needs and get them fulfilled. It is very common for a child to throw tantrums or behave rudely or inappropriately with their age norms. As a mom, it is important to realize that each time you react to unwanted behavior, you are recording them as thoughts in your brain. Whatever you converse to yourselves in your mind, while you are trying to change the child's behavior, you are reinforcing the same thoughts as impressions in your brain. This will create resistance within you. For example, you may think "Why do they do this to me?",

"What have I done to face this?", "Why do I deserve this kind of treatment, even after loving my child so much." These thoughts are repeated so often that they get deeply imprinted in your brain, just like a song that you learned in your childhood. Songs and rhymes that are repeated in your childhood get absorbed into your subconscious mind, and you can always recall or remember it at any time in your life. Similarly, you start to get into a default mode by unconsciously running these unhealthy, negative patterns in your mind. Next time even without the child's presence, you will worry and replay those thoughts, letting them sink deeper into your subconscious mind.

Now you understand the need to be conscious every time and how to avoid resistance. Resistance means thinking negative thoughts in your mind every time you face an unfavorable trigger. You are trying to control your child with negative thoughts and thus causing distress to yourself. This is another form of suffering. You are not only hurting yourself but also causing damage to your relationship with the child; most often, you end up rejecting the child. And a child who feels rejected will never cooperate or take steps to understand you.

In neuroscience, it is believed that each thought will secrete corresponding hormones that match the nature of your thoughts. If your thoughts are negative or unhelpful, they may release cortisol and adrenaline into your bloodstream. Each cell is now conscious of the emotion that is created. They get embedded into each cell based on your conscious mind's command. We have more than 70 trillion cells in our bodies. Each cell is similar to a soldier in an army. You are the master of this huge army, and these soldiers fight and serve for the benefit of your body. Each cell has its own consciousness and vibrates at a particular frequency. If the frequency of a cell is high, it means that the cell is healthier.

Just imagine a classroom of children who are not unified and cause chaos by shouting or crying. Every child behaves differently without any coherence. In that case, the teacher will definitely lose his/her control and may find it very difficult to manage the classroom. Similarly, if your cells are uncoordinated, the head of this army, the neocortex part of your brain (conscious mind), will have trouble managing the body. Only when all your cells are vibrating at a uniform frequency, the wavelength will be high enough to match what you think. Vibrations are the quality of energy stored in your cells. An unpleasant memory stored in a cell will have a lower frequency. How does this happen? Whenever you react based on what you think or feel about your child, every living cell in your body will record all those impressions. These impressions are later conditioned in your subconscious mind as programs. Since your subconscious mind dictates your life 95 percent of the time, your behavior may not match your intentions. Instead, it may be based on programs that are stored in your subconscious mind. And that is the reason why you hit your child unconsciously despite the fact you intend to be kind to them.

If you are a happy mom, you have a choice to respond and prevent subconscious reactions, as your reactive behavior will affect your state of peace. If you react, you can neither influence nor change your child's behavior. Now the most pressing question on your mind is "How can I change my child's behavior?" or "Is it even possible to change it? " Yes, it most certainly is. But, we'll take a look at it in the later sections.

You are constantly exposed to different challenges. Whether or not you get triggered by a challenging situation depends on your vulnerability. When triggered, only a loaded gun can shoot a bullet. Only a parent with a hurt inner child (bullet) will get hurt by their child's disrespectful behavior. When people's behavior doesn't meet your expectations, you react and interpret it based on your mental programs. Subsequently, the thought that arises in your mind is recorded in your brain as impressions. We believe that we can have a relationship only when we are constantly in touch with a person physically. The truth is the moment you come in touch with a person in life; you form a connection with them in your mind. If you notice, there is constant chatter in your mind whenever you think of that person. Although you are not in touch with them physically, your internal conversations have the power to make you feel good or bad about them. The thoughts you have about them are recorded in your brain simultaneously. It could be either positive or negative. When you think of someone negatively, you get affected. Naturally, a negative thought will create a neurochemical reaction that makes you feel unpleasant. So, even before you develop resentment towards someone, your mind and body get affected. These impressions are mostly repeated and recalled by your constant worrying throughout the day. What's more, they form new neural pathways in your brain. These neural pathways are reinforced every time you worry or even complain about a person. Slowly your attitude starts building up as you experience similar thoughts.

In my school days, whenever I saw my mom giving some extra fish to my brother, I gave it meaning instead of merely observing it.

I thought that my mother loved him more than me, which was not true. My mind was streaming these automatic thoughts from my core beliefs that I had imprinted in my subconscious mind earlier "I am not important." Every time I saw my mom doing something special for my brother, I replayed these thoughts over and over. What's more, I wasn't aware that these thoughts got etched into my brain. Since I did not use my intellect, I perceived what I believed rather than what I saw. My perception recorded a particular thought and reinforced it so many times so that it became a strong belief. Here, the belief that I kept on replaying and strengthening was "I am not valued or important."

This belief did not only become a part of my personality, but I also attached this belief to my self-image. Whenever I face an unfavorable situation, my reactions will be based on my self-belief. In fact, the situation could be as simple as my mom calling my brother for something,but my brain would immediately pop up the recording, "Oh, there she goes again,she loves him only,I am unimportant." So, the recording is what matters here. If my brain had reasoned out before recording it, my reaction would be different whenever I see my mom giving my brother special treatment.

It is observed that we start developing certain conditions around our inherent beliefs.In my situation, I had my own set of rules, "I am loved only if I am given priority." These rules maintain beliefs about myself and the world. Initially, you need to stop the recording. You can do this by noticing what you are telling yourself. Then, you need to reframe your thoughts rationally by questioning them. Once you start practicing this, you will observe the slowing down of your inner dialogues and thus reduce inner conflicts. As the number of inner conflicts you experience reduces, you will have more peace and calmness.

Motherhood – Breaks or Makes You

The necessity of your parental resources depends on two circumstances–the extent to which a child possesses the necessary resources, such as feeling connected, and the nature of the environment, whether it is challenging, conducive, or latent for the parent. If the mother faces both situations simultaneously, she would have trouble mobilizing her parental resources. If the child is born with a healthy temperament and environmental factors are conducive, then the mother can function at her best. When it comes to environmental factors, it also includes the spouse's role. The spouse needs to be sensitized to his wife's needs and must be in a position to offer necessary emotional support. But this does not always happen in every woman's life, as supportive life partners are pretty rare. Other environmental factors include even the financial status, family traditions, and family or work-life demands.

A child's hereditary characteristics and his/her past social experiences have the power to make or break their mental characteristics. When a child is emotionally deficient, he/she may seek parental resources. On the other hand, when a child is endowed with mental strength, the child will neither depend on his/her parents nor do parents influence their personality. However, not all mothers undergo struggles in their lives while raising their children. There are mothers who could raise their children without any hardships, thanks to a conducive environment that includes a supportive husband, adaptive extended family members, adequate family income, and the child's healthy temperament.

Temperament is a child's general behavioral pattern of how they react and interact with the environment. It is innate, congenital, and present from birth. Parenting is a herculean task. It is emotionally and intellectually exhausting and often demands professional sacrifices and subjects parents to serious financial hardships.

Parenting becomes tough due to either one of the two; the parent or child. All parents wish they had an easy baby. Parents who have difficult babies often envy those with calm ones. However, research shows that having a child with a difficult temperament is not all bad. Let's take a closer look at what temperament is all about. Once you understand these three types of temperament, we'll see what could be done if you have a difficult baby. Contrary to popular belief, a child's temperament is not based on genetics entirely. It is actually a result of biological and environmental factors which work together throughout a child's development since conception.

If you have more than one child, then you already know that each child is different despite being raised in the same home. Right from the beginning, newborns respond in adistinct style to their environment. Each infant has a unique temperament and personality type. Among the nine temperament traits, researchers found that six of them, namely activity, regularity, initial reaction, adaptability, intensity, and mood, cluster together to form three types of temperament. The three types of child temperament styles are:

- Easy temperament
- Difficult temperament
- Slow to warm up temperament

Needless to say, the problem arises only when parents are not aware of their own self in a deeper sense or if their child's temperament is difficult. The relationship between temperament and parenting is bidirectional. Difficult temperaments tend to elicit a tough response and inconsistent discipline from parents.

When a baby cries incessantly, you may have the urge to shout at them to stop. And when your difficult child yells at you, it is natural if you want to yell back. However, according to research, low emotional support, e.g., tough-love parenting, tends to raise children with mental health issues. Studies find that the mental well-being of people raised by authoritarian parents is often questionable. But you can often hear people who boast about being raised by tough parents and turning out fine. Why is there a discrepancy? This difference in resilience can be explained by the Diathesis Stress Model. According to the Diathesis-Stress Model, people who have a predisposition for psychological disorders have a lower threshold to trigger the disorder. Some difficult children have a worse disposition than others. When a difficult child who has a predisposition is parented by tough parents, they are more likely to develop psychological disorders. So providing tough love is simply not the answer to raising children with a difficult temperament. It can make things worse. Parents with fewer emotional baggage give birth to less problematic children. Irrespective of their temperament, kids are needy and demanding from the moment of their birth to… well, forever.

By remaining calm, responsive, and sensitive, it may take a long time to get through to your child. While the process is painstaking, the reward of being a happy parent is tremendous. There is no such thing as a good temperament or a bad temperament. Temperament by itself does not determine how a child will turn out; that is purely based on its cross-over interaction with the environment. Children with a difficult temperament are affected by parenting styles. They react more to the quality of parenting than easy children, for better and for worse. When raised with a good parenting style, a kid with a difficult temperament tends to do better in cognitive, academic, and social adjustment than their counterparts. On the other hand, when parenting is bad, a difficult baby will face a slew of emotional and mental problems when they grow up.

So feel blessed if you have a difficult or sensitive baby. Your difficult child actually has a better chance to succeed if you can provide good parenting. In most of the research studies on differential susceptibility, parenting quality is defined as good when parents display a high level of emotional and autonomy support. Bad parenting is when the parents display a low level of emotional and autonomy support. To reiterate, no parent is either good or bad; it is their parenting style that matters.

The mother is more than just a parent to her child. She is the one who carries the baby in the womb for 10 months, and even after she recuperates and adapts to changes on all magnitudes. It starts from her physiological, emotional, and social changes to other environmental factors, including her husband's support, financial situation, emotional support from family members, and more. While she may be prepared to celebrate her motherhood, her child's temperament and her own subconscious blind spots creep in, making her parenting bad. These blind spots are nothing but your own unhelpful thought patterns that are engraved in your subconscious mind. As the subconscious mind is full of hidden agendas, you may be unaware of these negative thought patterns. As the processing speed of the subconscious mind is 40 million times more powerful than your conscious mind, anything as small as a minimal change and unfamiliar situation can trigger your subconscious brain. Our brain always tends to find meaning in the stimuli or find out patterns that are familiar. We will talk about how our mind deals with unfamiliar instances in the future chapters.

Child is Your Guru: Learning Lessons from Your Children

How can your child be your guru? It may sound ridiculous, but to be honest, most parents learn valuable lessons from their children. Life is all about learning. When we stop learning, we stop evolving. As mentioned in the 2nd chapter, your script, aka mental programs (MP) in your subconscious mind, determines and runs your life. Are you aware of all the irrational beliefs in your subconscious mind? It is impossible as your mind is wandering most of the time. A simple way to handle this is to observe your thoughts when you interact with your children. You treat your child the way you treat your inner child. Your inner child is the combination of different emotions that you feel in your body. While it is easy to handle visible emotions with care, invisible or suppressed emotions are another story altogether. When you are unprepared to handle them, you become stressed and feel helpless as a mom.

To strengthen the intellect in your conscious mind, you need to consciously gain knowledge and skills. A better way to learn your mental programs is from your children. Children are a reflection of our inner self, a mixture of processed and unprocessed emotions. From the moment your child is born, they listen to all your happy, sad, angry, and bad stories. What's more, these stories are imprinted in their subconscious mind directly without any questions. Every time you feel sad or angry, you transfer the same vibration to your child's brain. Your mental programs will influence the way you treat or discipline your child. Mental programs are nothing but beliefs and stories that you keep telling yourself. These beliefs are indoctrinated into your child unconsciously.

When your child is a baby, you take care of them with unconditional love since you have zero expectations from them. Once the child becomes a toddler, you start to react based on expectations that you have towards them. Your expectation comes from your attitude. Your attitude is all about the rules and beliefs that you hold within yourself, consciously and unconsciously. These rules and assumptions are ingrained from your childhood. Your reactions are not caused by the child's misbehavior but by your conditioned default mind. If misbehavior is the cause, then all moms react the same way to their child's behavior. For example, not all moms react the same when a child spills food. Some of you may react very strongly because it is your expectation that dictates your behavior rather than the child's behavior. The child's behavior serves as only a trigger and not the cause. The cause is the rules and assumptions imprinted in your subconscious mind.

Let's assume that while you were growing up, one of your parents inculcated good food habits into you, insisting that you are a good girl only when you eat neatly or empty the plate. Eating neatly is a good value but not at the cost of being labeled as a good girl. Unknowingly you feel bad whenever you spill your food. You may feel guilty every time you waste food. You will not only blame yourself for not fulfilling those expectations, you will also get upset when you observe someone not following the rule.

The way you treat your inner child is reflected in your child. If you hate or dislike your emotional self, you will get upset the moment you observe emotional aspects in your child. This is not the same with others; you get affected by people whom you are attached (both securely and insecurely). When you are attached, it means you expect something from them to fulfill your emotional needs. That is when you form a bond. You will never expect anything from your friend or others, as you are not attached to them. When you place the obligation on others to satisfy your emotional needs, you suffer a lot. You get triggered easily. For example, when a mother insists on her child finishing the food, one child may obey and inculcate it into her/his subconscious mind, whereas the other child may resist and develop a power struggle with their mom. This difference is caused by their individual personality traits and genetic predisposition. It has nothing to do with your credibility as a good or bad mom. You react and respond based on your awareness levels and expectations. If you believe that children need to obey and submit to authority, then you may demand obedience.

When my daughter was a teenager, she loved to bake cakes and used to bake them in her free time. Once she finished her baking and left the place without cleaning. On that day, my servant had not turned up, and I had to do all the work. I requested her to sweep the floor and do some cleaning to make my work easier. She refused and didn't care about any of that. She was so engaged in her own work. I got very hurt inside. Instead of being assertive, I withdrew. My action was not caused by her behavior; my mental programs of feeling helpless and my expectations of her determined my reaction. The story I told myself was, "She is not being considerate to help me, which means she is not respecting me. As a mom, I am not able to make her do what I want, and it means I am helpless and cannot do anything." The thought that "I am a helpless mom" ruled my mind. In reality, I wanted to be a confident and proud mom. But, in this incident, my intention did not match my behavior. My daughter served as a trigger, and she was not the cause of my actions. She taught me to become the strong, confident mom that I am today, but it happened only after I became aware of my thoughts and actions.

> ***You can never be happy with your child, until you are happy without them.***

By noticing your behavior towards your children, you will slowly learn more about yourself. By learning more about yourself and your unconscious thought patterns, you can be a happy version of yourself.

Never Dream for Your Child, Dream for Yourself

It is the vision of every parent to see their child reach the peaks of success. However, it is a luxury that only a handful can afford. It is well known that high expectations can help children seek and achieve better results. One of the famous research works (Murayama) done among 12,000 students in the United States found that high parental aspirations led to increased academic achievement, but only when they did not remarkably exceed realistic expectations. When aspirations outshined expectations, the children's achievement decreased consistently. Murayama's study raises the question of how high is too high when it comes to expectations of a child's performance.

Are you a parent who is expecting too much that is incongruent with your child's capacity? It is very much true that having a positive thought about the child's abilities will definitely lead to a positive outcome. What matters here is the stance based on which you hold this belief about the child. The belief that you hold, "My child should succeed," should not be a projection of your unfulfilled wish. The child is not a commodity to fulfill all your unsatisfied desires. As a parent, it seems so natural to expect your child to fulfill or complete what you were unable to accomplish. But when you look at it from the child's perspective, it could be irrelevant and burdensome and subsequently lead to identity crises.

You need to allow your children to be themselves and not see them as extensions of yourselves to fulfill your dreams. You need to let your children live their dream, not yours.

My mom neither had a dream for her nor desired a dream for me. Her only expectation was to stay obedient and make her proud. That was a major detriment for me since it went against my personality traits. I was expected to listen to them and never disobey at any cost, which was impossible for a person like me. I was strong-minded and had an attitude to assess and question every belief before accepting it. Despite being an inherited trait, it was very much underutilized. The more I questioned my mom, the more she got disturbed and increased her demands for obedience. I woke up every morning and decided that from that day, I would

behave like a good girl by listening to my mom and living up to her expectations, but every time I failed spectacularly. With repeated negative cycles of this recurring thought, I broke down and couldn't bear the pain of not living up to my parents' expectations. That is when I wanted to leave this world and took an extreme step. I had swallowed some tablets (barbiturates) that I had with me for a neurological condition in my 9th class. It was my sister's birthday, and so we all left in a car to visit a nearby temple and go out to a movie. I had not disclosed this to anyone. I vomited while traveling in the car, and when my mom asked me about the vomiting, I revealed it to her. To my utter dismay, I got a nice hit on my head saying how stupid I was for doing something like this. At that moment, I told myself, "Oh my, they still don't love me." I had such a deep longing for love in my life. The irony of this was the very notion of gaining my mom's love was defeated. My emotional cup was always empty enough. The fortunate part was that they were supportive to take me to a well-known neurologist regularly to help me recover. Though my mom and dad loved me in their own way, the question was their misuse of power and unrealistic expectations.

As a parent, nothing is incomparable to accepting your child unconditionally. This could be unrealistic for any parent. Your insecure attachment style and identity crisis will restrain you from showing unconditional love to your child. The following section will elucidate the significance of unconditional acceptance of the child.

Unconditional Acceptance – the Key to a Healthy Relationship

How important is unconditional acceptance from parents, and why is it vital? It is a common question that everyone asks, but is it possible to accept a person as they are with zero expectations?

My answer is definitely yes. Initially, your child will look for your approval and acceptance. If not parents, it is important to have at least one adult, typically a mentor, who believes in the child for who they are. In my situation, it was my uncle (my dad's brother) who I call Appa. He was firm but kind to me and believed in me. His presence made a significant difference in my life. Another important factor that could help a child to develop self-belief is infusing spiritual practice into their life. In my life, as I studied in a convent, I had the habit of praying regularly. That habit helped me connect with my higher self, the infinite intelligence within me which guided me throughout my life. As a mom, you can discipline your mind through simple spiritual practices, such as praying every morning, keeping a gratitude journal, affirming positive words, simple breathing practices, and meditation.

In my childhood, I never felt accepted by my parents or other family members, except my uncle—my dad's brother. He showed me unconditional acceptance in small ways. When I was in my 9th standard, I got B grades in all my subjects. He told me, "I think you can get an A in all subjects next time." He instilled the seed of confidence in me irrespective of my misconduct which made me feel motivated and accepted. He saw something more in me that my parents couldn't. I am not here to say that my parents didn't love me or accept me. They were not able to match their actions with their intentions. They were too attached to me and had trouble aligning thoughts with their behavior. Due to their emotional dependency on me, they tended to react rather than respond appropriately. They were never taught to train their mind to take ownership of their feelings or tune their mind to be the person they want to be. It was my uncle's love and unconditional acceptance that gave me the strength to live in this world despite my depression and anxiety issues. He had expectations of me but was not dependent on me for

his state of mind. This is possible only when we use our intellect to guide our minds to remain stable and calm.

The moment you want to change your child, you are doomed. Yes, the intention to change your child comes from the belief that there is something wrong with your child. This implies that your child is defective from your perspective. Correcting your child's behavior is different from correcting them. You respect someone who perceives you in a very positive way. The best gift you could give your child is to perceive them as useful, capable, lovable, and powerful beings. This will make your child feel worthy and confident. The tricky part here is that only when you feel accepted with all your imperfections can you accept your child unconditionally. It is human nature to validate our worth based on how others look at us. It matters the most if you have very low self-esteem and a poor self-image. Unfortunately, most of us have low self-esteem. So, your perception will have a substantial impact on your child's success. Hence, it is imperative for you to choose your response carefully, irrespective of how your children behave. If you want to be a happy mom, naturally, your response will be kind, compassionate, and firm. This will subsequently invite your child to shift to their most resourceful state. When your relationship is built upon trust and love, your child will feel safe, secure, and accepted.

The next chapter is all about simple but powerful steps to tune your mind power. Using the power of the mind, you could start implementing these practices to become your best version. You will also find parenting skills and certain discipline tools that you could use aptly to get desired results.

POINTS TO PONDER:

1. To establish a happy mom and child (young adult) relationship, both of you need to feel self-sufficient and be respectful to each other.
2. If you are a happy mom, you have a choice to respond the way you want and prevent your reactive unconscious behaviour that will affect your state of peace. If you react, you can neither influence nor change your child's behaviour.
3. Temperament is a child's general behavioural pattern of how they react and interact with the environment. It is innate, congenital, and present from birth. The three types of child temperament styles are easy, difficult, and slow to warm up.
4. A better way to learn your mental programs is from your children. Children are a reflection of our inner self, a mixture of processed and unprocessed emotions.
5. You need to allow your children to be themselves and not see them as extensions of yourselves to fulfil your dreams. You need to let your children live their dream, not yours.
6. As a mom, you can discipline your mind through simple spiritual practices, such as praying every morning, keeping a gratitude journal, affirming positive words, simple breathing practices, and meditation.

* * *

Chapter V

The Seven Step Process to Create Your Happy Family

Chapter 5

The Seven Step Process to Create Your Happy Family

For one who has conquered the mind, the mind is the best of friends; but for the one who has failed to do so; the mind will remain the greatest enemy.

– Bhagavad Gita

In this chapter, you'll learn how to transform yourself to become a happy mom practically through a series of step-by-step processes. I would highly recommend you choose a diary or a book to journal your thoughts and carry out the activities given below.

1st Step: Redefining and Redesigning Your Self-Image

Each of us is endowed with a limited body and an unlimited mind. Using these two tools effectively, you can realize the true essence of who you are. You are the conscious awareness that operates the body and the mind. You are the awareness who looks out at the world through your six senses to gather all information and thereby giving meaning to each of them as they get encoded in your subconscious mind.

You need to know your true nature before learning anything in this world. Your core values define you. These core values only characterize you to be unique. Your core values are the fundamental aspect of life that decides your quality of life. Your values are your basic core beliefs that serve as the decisive force behind your attitude and actions. When you live a life that is aligned with your core values, your life will be more meaningful and beautiful. Suppose a person's core value is fun, then naturally, the person focuses on experiencing fun in their life to feel good.

The part that wants or aspires is the authentic and expanding portion of you called the evolutionary self. The part that fears and feels small and limited is your ego self. Whenever you are preoccupied with your ego self, you try to survive due to your attachment to it. Whereas, when you are in your evolutionary self mode, you will thrive to become the person you want to be. Identifying your core values will help you connect to the essence of who you are. It serves like a north star guiding you in the direction that you want to move forward.

The following exercise will help you identify your core values and evolve to your best version. Complete this written exercise and make a plan of how you will honour it in your day-to-day lives. This helps you find your true self and create a self-image that conserves your emotional stability.

Activity 1: Identify Your Core Values

Follow these 4 simple steps to identify your core values and how to inculcate them into your life to make it more meaningful.

1. **First, find a quiet place without any distractions and recall a perfect moment in your life. As you relive it in your mind, feel the emotions and elevate your vibration to match that moment.**

2. **Now, look into the list of core values (listed in the appendix) and choose any 10 that feel important to you.**
3. **Next, strike out five, which doesn't seem that important when compared to the rest.**
4. **Again, remove 2 more that seem unimportant comparably.**
5. **You are left with three core values.**
6. **Ask yourself how you will start to honour these core values. To what extent you will inculcate these values in your daily life.**

We all are born from pure unconditional love. No babies are born feeling not good enough. Self-image is how you see, feel, and picture yourself. Self-image is an idea in your mind. Indirectly, your self-image decides your life. Your self-image decides the results you get in life. If you want to change the results, modify the image you hold about yourself. If you want to become a happier mom, you have to become a happy version of yourself.

Activity 2: Recreate your self–image

- Do this exercise in your diary.
- Close your eyes, take a deep breath, and ask yourself,

"If I can have, do, be, say and create anything, what would I be doing? What is my deepest desire, and how would I feel if my desire is fulfilled? Who would it impact? Who do I want to be?"

- Open your eyes and connect to your heart's desire. Once you imagine it, write it down without any inhibitions. You will notice that you have created the best version of your own self. You need to think and act like the person that you want to be.
- Now you need to think and feel from the end state. If you want to be a confident mom, then you have to ask yourself, "What will I think, say to myself, feel, and do if I am a confident mom?"

So, think from the end and ask this question. Write down your answer clearly in descriptive terms.

- You need to picture yourself as a confident mom often in your mind to make your subconscious mind believe.

You need to make the mind believe, whatever you prefer it to believe, as it cannot differentiate between real and imaginary. The picture you hold in your mind will determine the way you feel and thus influence your behaviour.

Do this powerful exercise every day for 2 minutes: Surface emotions you will feel when you be your future self and teach your body to feel it often every day. The happy neuro-chemical released will circulate in your bloodstream and thus influence the cells in your body. This will modify the genetic expression of who you want to become. Do this for the next 30 days.

2nd Step: Be Tuned to Your Divine Inner Presence

You are not born alone. You (limiting, ego self) can never do anything alone. Maybe you can use your willpower to an extent, but you will still fail miserably in the long term. You need to tune to something more powerful (your higher self) than you. Why? There are a lot of miraculous things happening in our bodies. You have been breathing unconsciously all through your life. Your breath has been flowing in and out of your body, purifying it and keeping you alive. Moreover, millions of activities happen every moment in the 80 trillion cells of your body, whether you are aware of them or not. All these amazing things maintain harmony in your body throughout your life. Only an external source of energy that is present around the clock can keep these activities happening uninterruptedly to sustain your life. For all these physiological processes to happen continuously, you need expansive energy of consciousness. This powerful, expansive source of energy which is a luminous body can make you naturally feel safe, secured, and loved. This inner source of power is greater than any situation or problem you face. When you are in communion with this source, you will neither feel alone nor will your problems overwhelm you. This immense intelligence within you is beyond your senses, and you can experience it only on a deeper level of consciousness. This is your best companion. You are the experience of what you see, hear, taste, smell, and touch.

For a moment, close your eyes and notice what you see inside. You may see an inner world that is a reflection of your mind. If your mind is restless, you can never tune to the inner companion within you. It is essential to stay connected with this companion (inner light) that serves as an emotional GPS. On a daily basis, you need to be in touch with this inner silence to stay grounded and humble. It is very easy to get carried away by the external circumstances and demands that arise erratically in your external environment. Only by establishing a daily routine of practice can you keep in touch with this inner companion, which will ultimately provide you all the peace and happiness. Just like keeping your body clean and hygienic, you need to maintain your mental hygiene. A decision becomes worthless if you are not committed to it. Be committed to seeing the difference in you.

Here is a simple morning routine you can do. To remember the process, you can remember the word **ABCDE.** It is recommended that you do this just as you wake up before you get down from the bed, as the subconscious mind is more accessible during this time. You can also practice this routine after you finish your morning ritual.

ABCDE method for daily routine

A-Affirmation

The word, *am* is *ohm* in Sanskrit and is the language of our universe. Anything put after ohm becomes a reality. If we say it often, "I am tired," "I am stressed," it becomes a reality. If you are emotionally involved while saying this statement, it gets impressed into your subconscious mind. Whatever is impressed in the subconscious mind sets the vibration in your body. What you feel dictates your action and transforms it into a reality.

I am enough

I am peaceful

I am loved

I am happy

I am powerful.

I am secure.

This is what I want to be. This is who I am and what I am.

Process to imprint into your subconscious mind:

- After saying these mental commands silently in your mind, say the last sentence loudly from the bottom of your heart.
- Also, repeat any two, (I am enough is mandatory) throughout the day and every day for three weeks. Affirm this often with emotional involvement.
- In the second week, you will be able to get a mental picture in your mind spontaneously without your deliberate imagination.
- Only when you think (conscious mind) and feel (Subconscious mind) the same, you feel whole and complete without any internal conflict.
- This is done to lay the foundation and create space for new beliefs to be indoctrinated into your subconscious mind, or else the affirmations will never work for you.

Here are some powerful and useful affirmations that you can start to practice after you lay the foundation for three weeks.

> I am creating the life of my dream.
> Everything is working out for my highest good.
> All situations turn out to be good.
> I easily attract and manifest wealth and health into my life
> I have all happiness, health, success, and prosperity.
> I am so happy and grateful now that I am earning .....per month through my ....
> I am a magnet of abundance.
> I am grateful for boundless prosperity and blessings in my life.
> I am always receiving the flow of abundance, thank you, universe.
> All is well with me.
> Today is the day of miracles for me.

Here are two ways (Auto suggestions and hetero suggestions) you can indoctrinate the below affirmations into your subconscious mind.

1. First way is to read all these affirmations and read aloud with full emotional involvement. Secondly, record them on your mobile and listen to them every morning night going to sleep. Your voice must have great enthusiasm and joy.
2. Type and keep it as your mobile screen lock, paste in your cupboard or bathroom mirror, laptop screen, and as password for anything. This is reinforcing from outside environment.

B-Breath Work

Whenever you go to bed at a lower frequency with a disturbed or negative state of mind, then you will resume the next day at the same frequency. So, it is essential to raise your vibration when you get up.

After repeating affirmations, you need to take three deep breaths to align with your true self. Breath is the bridge that connects your body and mind.

C-Connect

Connect with the divine presence by bringing forth the image of your favorite god or something that symbolizes the inner companion within you.

D-Deep Gratitude

Your mind is a wandering machine. When you don't delegate any task to it, the mind will get cluttered easily. Creating new ideas is more important than nurturing your default thoughts. So, seeing the goodness in everything is the first step toward sound mental health. For this purpose, you can thank your parents, mentors, god, and this nature when you get up in the morning. ***Think of three things or people that you are very thankful for.*** This will definitely raise your vibration. This will never happen just by practicing for a week or month. It needs to become a habit of your lifetime. Think of your parents, friends, material possessions, body, qualities, skills and nature. Be grateful for each of them. This will integrate your thoughts and feelings. Only by thinking and freeing up your thoughts can you feel peaceful. The more integrated you are, the more you feel good.

E-Energy of Intention

The last and most important is setting your energy of intention. Write down 2-3 intentions in your diary when you set out for the day. These intentions will help focus your mind on what you want and align your thoughts with your feelings. They also serve as your roadmap to move forward in the right direction. You can write this in your diary as the first thing in the morning.

Example:

Today I will finish cleaning my cupboard/learn a new recipe/go to all my classes. (Doing)

Today I will feel calm/be grateful/be confident/appreciative/kind. (Being).

3rd Step: Allow Your Inner Self to Master Your External Environment

Your mind is a ship. Every ship has a captain, and in this case, it is your conscious mind, and the crew in the basement is your subconscious mind. The captain and crew have to coordinate and work together to get their desired results. The captain will lead by setting goals and by giving directions. The crew has to follow them so that they achieve what they aspire to. Now, if the crew is disconnected from the captain or the crew is lethargic and resents the captain, they will never co-operate, and so the mission is unaccomplished. The crew needs to stay happy and at ease to run the ship smoothly. When your subconscious mind is happy and relaxed, your body is in unison with what your conscious wants to achieve. When the captain and the crew work together, the outcome is a beautiful experience for everyone on board. You run the risk of water entering the ship when there is an internal problem within the ship or if the crew members don't follow the captain's guidance. It is important to keep the water from getting into the ship. Integrating your conscious mind and subconscious mind can help achieve that.

As you already know, the part of the mind that sets the goal is different from the part that executes the task. Your conscious mind (intellect) sets the goal it wants to accomplish, but it's the subconscious mind that carries out the tasks to achieve that goal. What you know (your intellect) does not control your behavior towards your child. You may know how to respond to your child, but what you do only decides your behavior. Now, you understand why you think something, but you have trouble executing it. Only by integrating your conscious mind with your subconscious mind can you achieve what you want. When you are not anchored with your own companion, you allow external situations (water) to affect you.

Here is the 4 step process to shift from your default, habitual mind to the focused conscious mind. The purpose is to release your unhealthy ego part, which obstructs your connection to your inner energy, your companion. Most of us suffer, not because of the crises we face, but because of our need to be in control of the situation or the people around us. When you feel safe and secure in your body and mind, you can focus on the present moment. In a nutshell, you need to practice how to shift from the default mode (subconscious mind) to the focused (Conscious mind).

Step 1: Observing and labeling your emotions

You need to observe the way you feel the emotion in your body without any judgment. When you experience these emotions, you will start to notice sensations in certain body parts. They are nothing but the pain you go through when these emotions show up in cells of that particular body part. Now label these emotions inside you. The more you use your intellect, the more you start to shift from subconscious mind to conscious mind. Tell yourself, "I am feeling bad/sad/afraid now." Take ownership of your feelings. Never blame your child for your emotions. Instead, try understanding how your child's behavior serves as a trigger to surface unhealthy memories in your subconscious mind.

Step 2: Shift from your subconscious mind to your conscious mind

With conscious awareness, you need to take a moment to notice your mind. You need to detach yourself and start observing what kind of thoughts arise in your conscious mind. You must know that not all thoughts are yours. Some of these thoughts are recorded data from your past. According to research, 95 percent of your thoughts are repetitive and come from your outdated database (past memories). Moreover, your reptilian complex, which serves as a survival mechanism to face the outside world, also puts you in a threatening mode. In order to feel safe and secure irrespective of any situation, you need to create a safe sanctuary within you and anchor yourselves to that state of being. Most of your emotional blockages are caused by a survival mentality. You need to choose thoughts that are helpful and supportive for you. In reality, you are 100 percent responsible for activating an unhelpful thought from the subconscious mind whenever a memory associated with it is reflected as a problem in your life now. Your child is only a stimulant that instigates your unprocessed, unpleasant memory.

Henceforth, don't get carried away with these thoughts that arise in your subconscious mind, the tape recorder. If you find it difficult, take deep breaths often to shift from your conscious mind to the observing mind.

Step 3: Use your imagination

Your mind is only a tool that serves you to achieve what you want. You must take measures to use it and not get carried away with it. The difficult part is that your mind thinks in pictures as it doesn't understand languages. Every thought is associated with an image. Whatever pictures are created in your mind become a reality. Your subconscious mind is a servant for you, which just accepts the image without any question and stores it. You can use this power in the right way. Instead of imagining anxious or sad pictures in your mind, you can consciously create pleasant and happy images. Once you create images that match your desired outcome, you start feeling good. Feeling good is the essence of creating a peaceful inner environment inside your mind. When your mind is peaceful, you can thrive anywhere in this world.

Step 4: Shift to the superconscious mind

When you are able to think and feel the same, and you are aligned with your core values, you are at peace even in an unfavorable situation. The only symptom that you are at the superconscious level is when you get new thoughts or ideas that make you feel peaceful and joyful.

To be mentally free is not just an overnight success; it's a process. If you remain undisturbed, even when you have the right to be upset, it means you have shifted to your superconscious mind. If your child misbehaves for some reason, you choose to respond from a state of inner calmness and awareness. If you take action from an agitated state, your action may not match your intentions.

Our emotions are an instrumental part of who we are, how we behave, and how we connect with our children. So being emotionally intelligent is necessary. IQ is said to explain only 20 percent of what we make of our lives.

4th Step: Shift from Scarcity Mindset to Abundance Mindset

Abundance is everywhere. Look around and notice. There is always plenty of air to breathe, but due to anxiety, you gasp for oxygen. There is plenty of water in the ocean, but still, our mouth feels dry due to fear. The environment is spacious, but you can feel cramped due to mental suffocation. You can be a part of a crowd but still, feel lonely if you are depressed. There are always more than enough resources available in our universe, but still, you turn your attention to what is missing and lacking from your inner world, the mind.

You are the scriptwriter. By now, you know that you have a script running in your subconscious mind, and what's more, you are living that script without evaluating it. As the director of the script, you can always choose to change the quality of the conversation in your head. That is the starting point to shift from a scarcity mindset to an abundance mindset.

Based on the law of attraction, the spherical law, whatever you think in your mind, is what you will get. It could be anything from a small needle to a huge universe. Everything comes down to the relationship that you have with that thing or the person. It is not about how you behave in the relationship. It is all about your thoughts and beliefs that decide the outcome you receive. ***You are what you think and not what others think!*** So, it is fundamental to notice and be conscious of the words you speak to yourselves, to others on the phone, to your relatives, friends, or children. Each word comes from the beliefs that you hold inside your subconscious mind. So be mindful while speaking and always narrate a story that supports your beliefs.

For example, let's consider a situation where your child disobeys you. You need to remember the time your child was cooperative and need to speak to others about them full of hope and optimism. You receive not what you want but what you expect from the state of an abundance mindset. Instead of complaining about their behavior, try saying this, "Yesterday, my child (focus on the goodness) was cooperative, and it made me feel more relaxed. I think he/she has the capacity to listen more."

Abundance is our birthright. When you notice the faults of your child, it will only lead to a scarcity mindset. Whereas, when you start to see the goodness in everything, including your child, you attract goodness into your life. Raising and being in the vibration of abundance is essential to feel sufficient and good inside. As your feelings decide your destiny, you need to ensure that you feel good irrespective of the situation around you. This may seem to be impossible at times, but by training your mind to stay calm and optimistic, you can master it.

There are two ways to maintain your vibration (the way you feel), one by feeling grateful and another is feeling appreciated. By practicing these simple rituals regularly, you can drastically reduce the chatterbox in your mind. With a minimal narrative in your head, you can experience peace in your mind.

Gratitude is the vibration of abundance.

Two methods to raise your vibration consistently:

Method 1: You can repeat statements repeatedly throughout the day, "Thank your favourite God name or Universe. "I feel blessed, I feel energised."

1. Keep an alarm for every one hour on your mobile from 9 am to 9 pm.
2. With every alarm, you need to take a deep breath and repeat these statements.

Method 2: The secret to feeling abundance is appreciation. The more you appreciate things or people around you, the more probable you are to shift to an abundance mindset. Set an intention one day to appreciate and admire things and people around you. You will feel the difference. You will feel very good inside, as you will surpass the data of your subconscious mind and connect with the magnificent source of universal power.

When you drop the **3Cs** mentioned below, you can shift to a state of appreciation.

Complaining to others: Take a moment now and decide to stop talking about what is missing in your life and instead focus on what you are blessed with.

Criticizing self and others: Rather than blaming yourself or others for your emotions, decide to appreciate the goodness in everything, especially in a negative situation.

Comparing ourselves with others: Stop a moment and take a firm decision to stop comparing yourself with anyone. Compare only with your own progress. This is the best way to honor and love yourselves.

By eliminating these 3Cs from your life, you can definitely increase your vibration and feel more vibrant and happier.

5th Step: Decide Your Emotional Signature

This is the most important step as this decides the destiny of your life. Your emotional signature is the frequency at which you will vibrate all day long in your life. If you get influenced by external situations and people, your emotions will be inconsistent and will ultimately affect your vibration. Emotional intelligence (EQ) is more significant than intellectual intelligence (IQ).

According to Daniel Goldman, emotional intelligence includes four main skills, namely, self-awareness, self-management, social awareness, and relationship management. You can help your child identify and manage their own emotions. While you are at it, help them acknowledge their feelings and understand the impact of these emotions on themselves and their relationships. By creating your own emotional signature, you can help your child to achieve a high EQ. For this purpose, you need to master your emotional signature.

The quality of the emotions you feel day-to-day decides your quality of life. So, being aware of your emotions is the first step in taking charge of your life and being happy. To manage your emotions properly, you need to be aware of them first. Further, you need to understand and empathize with how your child feels to manage the relationship with your child.

Follow these 4 steps to manage your own emotions.

Step 1: Choose one area of your life that you are unhappy with.

Example: Money, relationships, career, health, and spirituality.

Step 2: Draw two columns. Write down all your negative thoughts in the left column.

Step 3: Write a counter thought in the right column for every negative thought.

Step 4: Read the right column aloud as often as possible to reinforce new thought patterns in your subconscious mind.

If you look closely, you will notice that all these negative thoughts will either be ghosts of your past or a fear of your future. If you continue to think this way, you will keep living in the past. Instead of focusing on the problems, you need to concentrate on what you want instead. Write down what you want to happen in every specific area of your life.

Choose one wish that you want to turn into reality. Write down what kind of a person you want to be to achieve your goals.

If you choose a relationship, then you will need to focus on how you want to behave and how you want the child to treat you so that you can maintain a boundary.

Ask yourselves this question, "Why do I want this in my life?" Find at least 2 to 3 strong positive reasons for this wish to manifest. These reasons will definitely motivate you.

A disturbing thought or emotion is an unhealed part that is separated from your core self. It is essential to heal any emotion that arises in your body immediately, as it may become a mood that slowly turns into temperament and then ultimately embedded into your personality. You know very well now that your personality creates your personal reality.

The ho'oponopono method is a powerful exercise that can be used when you feel helpless and indifferent and take any action momentarily. This technique can be used as a preventive method to make your relationship better and healthier. When used in difficult situations, this technique has proven to be very effective in healing relationships and other problems.

Ho'oponopono Technique

The word ho'oponopono means to correct a mistake or make things right to strike a balance. This is an ancient Hawaiian practice of forgiveness that serves as both a communication concept for a reunion and an instrument to restore self-love and balance in your life. You need to understand certain concepts before inculcating this practice into your life.

The entire world is your creation. You may find this difficult to accept. Let us simplify this further. The world is like a mirror. Whatever you see outside is the reflection of something within you. If you are hurt, you will meet people or family members who experience the same.

You can take total responsibility for things that happen within you. You may wonder how do I take responsibility for things that happen in the environment? You know that everything is energy. The world, which now has a population of 8 billion, initially had just one human being. This one human being who was full of energy then proliferated into hundreds, thousands, lakhs, millions, and billions. According to the Law ofDivine Oneness, you are a part of a whole. Whatever you observe outside is activating a wave of anxiety, sadness, or anger in your subconscious mind. You need to get rid of this habit, and that is the premise of this technique. So, you need to make some internal changes to see the change outside. You must constantly clean unpleasant memories in your subconscious mind.

This method helps release the mental programs embedded in your subconscious mind. Let us see how it happens. More than a million thoughts arise in your mind every day. You are aware of a tiny (5 percent) fraction of these thoughts. When a thought arises, it activates a memory associated with it from your subconscious mind. This becomes a problem in your life. Problems are memories that reappear throughout your life. Once you know that you are 100 percent responsible for all that happens in your life, you can accept the difficulties you face and make an attempt to remove them from your life.

You turn to universal energy to appeal as it knows your blueprint to heal your thoughts and emotions. You will never know what activated the memory and turned it into a problem. The trigger (your child's behavior) from the environment will provoke suppressed emotions in your subconscious mind. By practicing this method regularly, you can clean your subconscious mind and thus feel more peaceful and organized inside. This will enhance and improve your quality of life.

Sit in a place and bring your child or another person in front of your mind. Focus on yourself and repeat each statement three times to the universe. Never say these statements from a state of guilt, but always from a state of love and compassion for the person in your mind's eye.

I'm sorry...to experience this problem in my life. I am sorry for being unaware and activating this memory. I am sorry for my role in creating this.

Please forgive me...for not being aware of this. I am willing to let it go and release these painful memories.

Thank you...for this problem in my life and for the chance to clean it. Thank you for releasing me and solving my problems.

I love you...for having this opportunity to cleanse my mind. I know I am a part of the divine.

You can also repeat just these 4 short statements whenever a negative emotion arises in you. Doing this regularly cleanses your mind and makes it peaceful. You need to understand certain things clearly to get the best results.

- Everything that seems to happen out there is actually happening in your mind.
- Whatever happens to you is a reflection of some unresolved and unprocessed emotions that linger within you.
- You are 100 percent responsible for whatever you face in your life.
- Whenever you undergo some distress, it means that your subconscious mind needs a thorough cleansing.

When you have a negative feeling, honour it and feel it fully. Don't ever try to run away from it or control it. It is okay to feel negative emotions as long as you are aware of their true nature. Be willing to witness the emotion without any judgment and be full of love. Not all thoughts that arise in your mind are your thoughts. Only when you give your attention to thought and believe it do you fall into the trap.

6th Step: Rewrite Your Mental Programs

Your mental program is a conditioned belief in your subconscious mind that controls all your unwanted yet habitual behavior. 90 percent of your behavior is in autopilot mode, which hails from your identity-based persona. Now, you need to reprogram your subconscious mind as you are not aware of what limiting beliefs you hold inside. These limiting beliefs prevent you from experiencing your true nature. These mental programs control the relationship with your children, sway your behavior towards your children, decide the effectiveness of your parenting and ultimately determine your quality of life. If you want to change your life, you need to change your mental program.

There are two ways to rewrite your mental program. The first idea is through affirmations—repetition with an infusion of emotions. Some powerful statements, when repeated, go into your subconscious mind and override your existing unhelpful programs. The second option is using your conscious mind to be mindful. In this method, you can reframe your thoughts immediately after you notice them. Bonus tip: start using humor as your way of life.

Repetition of an idea with emotional fusion is an easy yet compelling technique. To execute it, you need to decide what you want and ask yourself why you want it. You should have a strong reason for wanting it. It should be something that gives you exuberant motivation and power.

When I started to write a book in 2020, I stopped writing after a few chapters and kept procrastinating. It was not because of my laziness or lack of motivation but solely due to the fact that I lacked a strong reason. When I started doing this exercise, I found one meaningful reason. I wanted to stop the suffering of every mom and empower them. I wanted every mom who picked this book to know the secrets and simple, practical ways to overcome their internal suffering. This reason caused quite a stir within me.

Follow the exercise given below to reprogram your subconscious mind. For this, you need to come out of your comfort zone and stop feeling the same way every day. Instead, you need to feel the emotion you want so that you can rise beyond the circumstances. Everything that happens in your life prepares you for who you want to become. For this purpose, you need to understand your mind and work in harmony with universal laws to intentionally create a relationship you want with your child. The infinite energy source within you will help you achieve what you want and guide you to become who you want to be. Practice the mirror exercise every day in the morning to remind yourself that you are good enough irrespective of everything that has happened in your life. Feeling mindful and good is important to becoming a happy mom.

a) Mirror Exercise

1st step: Feel Good

Stand before the mirror. Look into your eyes in the mirror. Ask the person in the mirror, how are you? Get in touch with your innate emotions. (Be honest). If you are not feeling good, shift your vibration to feel good. Repeat your affirmations and infuse emotions into them.

2nd step: Repeat Eternal Phrases

When you start with a why, you can easily bypass the inner critical voice in your head. For example, if you want to become confident, there will be resistance like "no you are not". Instead, think of one situation or memory that displayed your confidence and say "Why am I so confident in speaking to strangers", "How do I handle my kids so confidently?"

Other examples:

- Why am I so loved by everyone?
- Why does my husband always understand me?
- How am I always so kind to my children?
- Repeat these thoughts and pump them fully with emotions.

b) Gratitude Letter:

Instead of living in the past, you need to envision the person you love to see yourself as. Imagine your future self and see the person you want to become in six months. Write a letter to the universe, feeling grateful and blessed for fulfilling all your desires. When you are writing to the universe, thank it for all the good things that will happen in your life and feel it fully in your body. While writing the letter, picture your desires becoming a reality in your mind and your subconscious mind will not only affirm it but also eventually make it happen.

7th Step: Discipline Methods and Strategies to Handle Your Children

Not all discipline methods are based on punishing or expressing righteous anger toward your kids. There are a ton of ways in which you can guide and teach your children while holding a firm ground. Here are some effective disciplining methods that you can learn to apply consistently with your children ranging from toddlers and pre-teens to teens and young adults, to modify their behavioral problems.

Discipline Methods

I) Communication Skills

A) Connecting Skill

B) Nonviolent Communication

A) Connecting Skill

How to connect before correcting the child's behavior

Look into your child's eyes directly and converse

- **Become mindful. Shift to your evolved self.**
- **You are feeling................because ....**
- **You wish.........**

Let us consider this example. Assume that your daughter was upset when she returned from school and complained about her friend not playing with her. Usually, we tend to ask, "What did you do? Why did they ignore you?"

Instead, you can try this, "you seem to feel very upset and maybe sad because your friend didn't include you. You wish she had joined you in the play."

This display of empathy helps you build a bond with the child more easily and comes in handy while discussing the issue later.

B) Non-Violence Communication (NVC TOOL)

One of the communication tools that I would like to share here is nonviolent communication by Marshall Rosenberg. When you get disturbed or hurt for any reason, you can use this NVC tool to express your thoughts and feelings to your child without blaming them. Depending on your child's relationship with you and their resources, you will arrive at a plausible outcome. You cannot expect them always to do what you want, but you can draw a boundary for them to clarify your expectations.

Here's a 4 step process that you can use to express your needs and feelings appropriately with your child.

1) Observation

   State the observations that make you say something. Stay free of judgments, labels, diagnosis, and opinions.

   Example "It is 4 am and I can see you watching TV." This states an observed fact, while "It is too late, you are not obeying me" is a judgment.

   "When I see/hear/notice…"

2) Expression of feelings

   State the feeling that the observation triggers in your body.

   "I feel ……………"

3) Express your needs

   State the unmet need that is causing the emotion, towards your child.

   "...Because I need/value ..."

4) Request

   This needs to be free of demands; make a concrete request for action to fulfill a justified need.

   "Would you be willing to...?"

NVC SKILL
When I see/hear/notice..................
I feel..
Because I need.............................
Would you be willing to..................

II) Behaviour Management Skills

These methods are adapted from Alfred Adler's disciplinary model. He was the first social psychologist to mention social interest. One of the primary indicators of a healthy mind is a person who has a social responsibility and social interest. You can discipline your child only when they are willing to cooperate. Without their permission, you can never make them do anything. Once they reach the age of 7, your child will have their own emotional GPS (inner guidance), and you need to allow them to use it. Being a happy mom, you will be privileged to respond with mindfulness. As you know, setting an intention before you expect anything from your child is more important. With this awareness, you need to operate from a resourceful state instead of a stressful state.

A) **Logical Consequence Method**

This method is used when your child is engaged in unwanted behavior, and you want to stop or modify it. Usually, the child will face natural consequences that you don't need to interfere with. In certain situations, you need to intervene when the results are severe. If your child is not studying properly, ignoring them will lead to a natural consequence of failed exams. So, you need to intervene and provide them with a logical consequence. After discussion, you may choose a respectful, reasonable, relevant consequence to their misbehavior and reveal it earlier (4R). Implementing the consequence with the 4R criteria is significant as it decides your desired outcome. If it's not implemented accurately, the child will feel punished.

Example: Your child is leaving their clothes strewn across the floor in their room.

You can inform them earlier that if they don't deposit their clothes into the laundry basket, their clothes will remain unwashed, and they have to wash it themselves.

The child must act appropriately as they know the consequences they will face. Instinctively they need to choose what they want to do. This ensures that they start using their inner guidance system to set out their path of action. This makes them responsible.

B) **Problem-Solving Skill**

Short method: WW (Win-Win) Method.

Where to use: In a quick situation (Shopping mall, market, or other outdoor settings)

Instead of arguing with your child, have a healthy discussion.

I think/feel.....

You think/feel....

What can we do?

If they are not willing to cooperate for some reason, you can follow up later.

Long method: WW method

When to use: When there is a long-time conflict that is unresolved between both of you. Whenever there is a power struggle between you and your child, regarding study, phone, time, food, dress, or play.

Long WW Method: A8 Step Process

1. **Ask**

   I have been observing you for some time.... (Mention something very specific in anon-judgmental way)

   Can we speak about...? (if they say no, ask about their availability and set an appropriate time).

2. **Mention the issue you observed**

   Example: "I hear you saying bad words while playing and I want to talk about it as it's not helpful. Can we solve it now? Are you fine talking about it?"

3. **Express how they feel**

   Listen to your heart even if your mind disagrees.

   Example: I know you are not aware of the meaning of those words. Inherently, you don't want to speak those words but still end up speaking them without your control.

4. **Express how their actions affect you and how you feel**

   You need to notice your feelings and convey them to your child honestly. Do not use this opportunity to manipulate or blame them. You are just honoring yourself by being truthful.If your child loves you very much and is conscious enough they will cooperate.

5. **Ask what we can do**

   Put the ball in the centre. It is not about who is right or who is wrong. It is about what is right or how to make it right.

6. **List out options together**
   First ask the child (age 5 and above) to think of all options and then pitch in lastly with one or a couple more options.
7. **Choose one option from the list**
   Your child only has to choose the option which is possible for them. As they were informed earlier about plausible consequences, they will be responsible and committed to making a choice.
8. **Decide logical consequences**

This has to be done mutually. Your child only have to decide the consequence. If its not possible, you need to get their permission for the consequence you had chosen. The consequence needs to be

- Revealed in advance.
- Respectful for the child.
- Related to the offence.
- Reasonable for your child.

Example: If you speak bad words, you must repeat good ones. Or, you need to write down affirmations.

Try using this method once and see the results for yourselves. If they are unwilling to cooperate, work on establishing a relationship before implementing these methods.

C) **Encouragement Skill**

Adler says the only disease that humans suffer is discouragement. Encouragement is the only antidote for it. Every child is nurtured by the environment they are raised in. According to epigenetics, you know that a very supportive home environment will impact the child's personality and, in turn, determine the genetic expression. One of the best ways to influence your child's behavior is through encouragement. When are you happy? When someone appreciates or acknowledges your behavior, you feel encouraged and good. This will enhance your self-image and subsequently increase your self-esteem. Self-esteem is one of the solid indicators of your child's mental well-being. When your child performs something that is not up to your expectations, you either be critical or give a superfluous comment. It is important to give the child an authentic appreciation that is helpful.

Encouragement is a powerful tool for building your child's personality. It would help if you appreciated your child whenever they did helpful and good things. Instead of focusing on what is wrong, you need to see the goodness in them. This is an art that you need to develop.

Example: Your child (Any age) has not completed the 10 math sums you asked them to do.

You could say, "I noticed that you took the effort to finish the first 3 sums. It shows that you are good at this. Maybe you could complete the rest similarly."

Use these 3 steps always to appreciate and encourage your child.

Encouragement Skill

- **Tell a positive feedback**
- **Appreciation should be very specific**
- **Point out the resources that you notice in your child**

Bonus: Don't Use Mindfulness as a Technique; Make it a Way of Life

95 percent of the time, you are living in automation, i.e., you are not conscious of your thoughts and emotions. Since you are in automation, mechanically negative emotions only will arise in your mind. Negative thoughts will make you suffer and drag your energy down. When you are mindful, you can tune your mind and create new experiences. This will override your automated negative thoughts and make your subconscious produce positive thoughts automatically. When mindful, you can choose to respond appropriately or not to respond sometimes.

Whenever you feel low, use this 3R method to practice mindfulness.

Recognize- Identify and label the emotion that you experience in the body

Reframe- Identify the thoughts associated with this emotion and look at the situation from a different perspective

Release- Take 3 deep breaths and release the emotion. You can imagine the emotion washing away from your body or exiting your body in the form of black smoke.

POINTS TO PONDER:

1. Your core values define and characterize you. Your core values are the fundamental aspect of life that decides your quality of life. When you live a life that is aligned with your core values, your life will be more meaningful and beautiful.
2. The inner source of power you hold within you is greater than any situation or problem you may face. When you are in communion with this source, you will neither feel alone nor will your problems overwhelm you.
3. You need to shift from your default, habitual mind to the focused conscious mind. The purpose is to release your unhealthy ego part, which obstructs your connection to your inner energy, your companion.
4. As you are your own scriptwriter, you can always choose to change the quality of the conversation in your head. That is the starting point to shift from a scarcity mindset to an abundance mindset.
5. The quality of the emotions you feel day-to-day decides your quality of life. So, being aware of your emotions is the first step in taking charge of your life and being happy.
6. The ho'oponopono method helps to release the mental programs implanted in your subconscious mind.
7. Your mental programs control the relationship with your children, affect your behaviour towards your children, decide the effectiveness of your parenting and ultimately determine your quality of life. If you want to change your life, you need to change your mental programs.

* * *

Final Thoughts

Disorder is the order of the universe. Yes, this world is not in order. Chaos and injustice prevail in this universe. We have stepped into this disorderly world not to fix the world but to cleanse our minds and become pure humans who are filled with love and light. Why does a student go to school? To enjoy or to suffer?To play or to get a degree? Students enroll in a school to study and become better individuals. They don't aspire to change how the school is run but to become more knowledgeable and skilled. The school serves as a medium to help people evolve into learned and educated people. The world is not a place of disease….it's our mind that gets corrupted. A diseased mind can never feel healthy in a body. Our mind gets easily distressed when we have an expectation. This is conditioned by the environment we live in during our childhood. When we realize this, we can break free from all our past conditioning programs in our subconscious minds.

You know that 95 percent of your brain is a record of all your past memories and emotions associated with them. What if you live with the same emotions that have defined you for the past 10 to 15 years? Your brain doesn't know the difference between the actual experience which creates the emotion and the emotions elicited by replaying a thought. Never live in the past. Your body will become the memory of all painful emotions that you experienced in the past. You can never feel good when you live with past conditioning. You will limit yourself if you continue to live in the past. So it is imperative to not only be very mindful in choosing your response to your child but also to reform and modify your limiting beliefs, which reside under the unhelpful emotions that arise in challenging situations.

If you want to see a change in your relationship and feel happy about yourself, you need to think and feel beyond your environment. With the new knowledge of epigenetic science, it is found that the way you perceive, irrespective of the environment, either favourably or unfavourably matters very much. It can alter your genetic expression without changing the genetic code.

Each mom has her own powerful inner guidance system which guides her actions accurately. But, unfortunately, most mothers, when they face a demanding situation, fall back into their default autopilot mode and react (her own inner parent) the way their minds were conditioned to. In any given situation, either the parent or child has to take their own stance on how they could use their evolving impulse rather than resorting to egotistical actions which could only damage their relationship. In any situation, the parent or child needs to ask themselves how they could be a part of the solution in any way that is helpful for the situation instead of finding faults and taking on a defensive stance.

Being a happy mom is not your destination, as it is short-lived. Playing a mom's role is necessary only until your child becomes an adult. Your child as an adult needs a person who could be available as a mentor, friend, advisor, or buddy. They can parent or re-parent themselves. If you choose to continue living the mom role, your child will continue living as a child. The choice is yours.

It is said that mothers are a symbol of pure love and they are selfless beings. It is a parable that all mothers are embodiments of selfless love. Not all moms in this world can be selfless. Your love for your child depends upon your self-happiness. This may seem outrageous. The truth is true love is not so easy to experience. As a mom, you may sometimes be selfless, but not always. Why?

As a human being, you indulge in acts to seek your own happiness. This happiness depends on your self-interest. If your interest is fulfilled, then you feel happy. When you are happy, you feel loved inside. Only when you feel loved can you shower love on your child. Eventually, you will feel unhappy and unloved if your self-interest is at stake. When your self-interest is fulfilled your child looks like a good child. When your self interest is not fulfilled, then your child becomes a bad child. For example, if your child has trouble succeeding in exams, one of the important priorities for your happiness, you cannot love your child as your self-interest is obstructed. Also, your self-interest is at stake when you feel depressed about something else. You may feel emptiness, loneliness, or emotional pain that makes it very difficult to connect with or love your child. Looking from this perspective, you come to understand that love is an emotion that's experienced by self and not in a relationship. So, taking care of and fulfilling your interest is essential to keep yourselves happy.

True love does not depend on the fulfilment of your self-interest. True love is when your sole focus is the happiness of your child. This will be a challenging task for moms searching for their own happiness. Essentially, this is the reason is why being a happy mom will uphold you to a state of giving love for your child selflessly.

You create your own reality by not what you think but what you feel about it. It is not about what runs continuously in your mind, but everything about how you constantly feel in your day-to-day life. Your emotions decide your life's destiny. So being a happy mom is more important in deciding the quality of your relationship with your child.

Being a happy individual is the key to being a happy mom. You can give your child all of the love in the world, but if you're not feeling good about yourself, it will be difficult for them to feel good as well. The processes shared in this book are essential for self-care and self-love. If you take care of yourself first, you will have more to give your family. I hope you found the book insightful and enlightening in finding your true self.

The End

* * *

Bibliography

American Psychological Association, Multitasking: Switching costs Subtle "switching" costs cut efficiency, raise risk, March 20, 2006

Chris Wodskou, (2022),Uncertainty and complementarities are core principles of the subatomic world and maybe in ours as well,Posted: Mar 03, 2022.

Clifford Nass, (2013) https://www.medindia.net/news/research-finds-that-multi-tasking-is-bad-for brain-and-makes-you-an-incompetent-worker-118041-1.htm

Elissa S. Epel, Eli Puterman, JueLin,Elizabeth Blackburn, AlanieLazaro, WendyBerryMendes,WanderingMindsandAgingCells(2013),Clinical Psychological Science 1(1):75-83, DOI:10.1177/2167702612460234

Ethan Siegel, Starts With A Bang, (2020), In Quantum Physics, Even Humans Act as Waves.https://www.forbes.com/sites/startswithabang/2020/08/19/in-quantum-physics-even-humans-act-as-waves/

GözdeGökçe, banuyilmaz,Emotional Availability of Parents and Psychological Health: What Does Mediate This Relationship? March 2018, Journal of Adult Development 25(1):37-47, DOI:10.1007/s10804-017-9273-x

Hazan C.; Shaver P.R. (March 1987). Attachment styles in adults: "Romantic love conceptualized as an attachment process". J PersSoc Psychol. 52 (3): 511–24.

Infant temperament predicts personality more than 20 years later: Behavioral inhibition in infancy associated with introversion and internalizing psychopathology in adulthood, April 20, 2020,NIH/National Institute of Mental Health.

Lipton, B. (2005). ***The Biology of Belief: Unleashing the Power of Consciousness, Matter & Miracles.*** Santa Rosa, CA: Elite Books,

Gabor Filo DDS, FAGD, ABHD, Page 353 Published online: 21 Sep 2011

Lipton, Bruce H.. *The Biology of Belief: Unleashing the Power of Consciousness, Matter & Miracles.* 10th anniversary edition. Carlsbad, California: Hay House, Inc, 2016. Print.

Kelly Gonsalves & Kristina Hallett (2021) https://www.mindbodygreen.com/articles/attachment-theory-and-the-4-attachment-styles.

Miriam K Forbes, Ronald M Rapee, Anna-Lisa Camberis, Catherine A McMahon (2017), Unique Associations between Childhood TemperamentCharacteristicsandSubsequentPsychopathologySymptom Trajectories from Childhood to Early Adolescence,45(6):1221-1233. doi: 10.1007/s10802-016-0236-7.

Qudsia Anjum Fasih, (2018) Women are hard-wired to be stronger. From physiology to psychology, women have the advantage over men, says expert Published:January 26, 2018.

Richard Davidson on Why Awareness Is Important to Our…(2021) https://www.theawakenetwork.com › dr-richie-davidson.

Rosenberg, Marshall B. Nonviolent Communication: A Language of Compassion. Del Mar, CA: PuddleDancer Press, 1999. Print.

Science of the Heart: Exploring the Role of the Heart in Human Performance, An Overview of Research Conducted by the Heart Math Institute, Chapter 06: Energetic Communication. https://www.heartmath.org/research/science-of-the-heart/

Steven Stoncy, The Uncertainty Principle in Relationship Dynamics: There's a way to use it for better connection, Posted April 14, 2021

Susan M. Henney, (2016), Wandering Minds and Aging Cells January 2013, Clinical Psychological Science 1(1):75-83, DOI:10.1177/2167702612460234

Appendix

Know your Adult Attachment Style Mini-Questionnaire

Instructions:

When completing this questionnaire, please focus on ONE significant relationship – ideally a current partner as the focus here is on adult relationships. This does not *necessarily* need to be a romantic relationship but *must* be the individual with whom you feel the most connection.

This questionnaire is designed to be an interactive learning tool. When responding, consider how strongly you identify with each statement – disagree, mostly agree, strongly agree. Using the scale below, respond in the space provided.

Disagree	Sometimes Agree	Mostly Agree	Strongly Agree
0	1	2	3

Secure

1. I feel relaxed with my partner most of the time.
2. I find it easy to flow between being close and connected with my partner to being on my own.
3. If my partner and I hit a glitch it is relatively easy for me to apologize, brainstorm a win-win solution, or repair the misattunement or disharmony.

4. People are essentially good at heart.
5. It is a priority to keep agreements with my partner.
6. I attempt to discover and meet the needs of my partner whenever possible and I feel comfortable expressing my own needs.
7. I actively protect my partner from others and from harm and attempt to maintain safety in our relationship.
8. I look at my partner with kindness and caring and look forward to our time together.
9. I am comfortable being affectionate with my partner.
10. I can keep secrets, protect my partner's privacy, and respect boundaries.

Section Total

Avoidant

1. When my partner arrives home or approaches me, I feel inexplicably stressed - especially when s/he wants to connect. 2. I find myself minimizing the importance of close relationships in my life.
3. I insist on self-reliance, have difficulty reaching out when I need help and do many of life's tasks or my hobbies, alone.
4. I sometimes feel superior in not needing others and wish others were more self-sufficient.
5. I feel like my partner is always there but would often prefer to have my own space unless I invite the connection.
6. Sometimes I prefer casual sex instead of a committed relationship.
7. I prefer relationships with things or animals instead of people.
8. I often find eye contact uncomfortable and particularly difficult to maintain.
9. It is easier for me to think things through than to express myself emotionally.

10. I act like I don't need reassurance or encouragement when sometimes I, in fact, do.
11. When I lose a relationship at first I might experience separation elation and then become depressed.

Section Total

Anxious/Ambivalent

1. I am always yearning for something or someone that I feel I cannot have and rarely feeling satisfied.
2. I am more prone to feeling sorry for myself when I have a problem than to take action and solve it.
3. Sometimes, I over-function, over-adapt, over-accommodate others, or over-apologize for things I did not do.
4. I feel like I over-focus on others in general and tend to lose myself in relationships.
5. It is difficult for me to say NO or to set realistic boundaries.
6. I chronically second-guess myself and sometimes wish I had said something differently.
7. When I give more than I get I often resent this and harbor a grudge. It is difficult to receive love from my partner when they express it.
8. It is difficult for me to be alone. If alone, I feel abandoned, hurt, and angry.
9. I feel a deep wish to be close along with a paralyzing fear of losing love of the relationship.
10. I want to be close with my partner but feel angry at my partner at the same time. Sometimes I pick fights when my partner shows up when we go on a "long awaited for" vacation.
11. I want to be close with my partner but feel angry at my partner at the same time.

Section Total

<u>Disorganized:</u>

1. When I reach a certain level of intimacy with my partner, I sometimes experience inexplicable fear.
2. When presented with problems, I often feel stumped and feel they are irresolvable.
3. I have an exaggerated startle response when others approach me unexpectedly.
4. My partner often comments or complains that I am controlling.
5. I often expect the worst to happen in my relationship.
6. I struggle to feel safe with my partner. Protection often feels out of reach.
7. I have a hard time remembering and discussing the feelings related to my past attachment situations. I disconnect or dissociate and get confused.
8. Stuck in approach-avoidance patterns with my partner, I want closeness but am also afraid of the one I desire to be close with.
9. I override my instinctive self-protective responses when possible danger is present – sometimes feeling immobilized, disconnected, or "gone".
10. I am easily confused or disoriented, especially when stressed. It is important for my partner to keep arrangements simple and clear.

Section Total

<u>Scoring:</u> The section with the highest number will likely correspond to your unique attachment style. You may discover a dominant style or a mix of styles. This questionnaire is not meant to be a label or diagnosis. It is only intended to indicate tendencies and prompt more useful, precise personal exploration.

Core value Sheet Exercise

Core Value	Not Important	Important	Extremely Important
Authenticity			
Achievement			
Adventure			
Authority			
Autonomy			
Balance			
Beauty			
Boldness			
Compassion			
Challenge			
Citizenship			
Community			
Competency			
Contribution			
Creativity			
Curiosity			
Determination			
Fairness			
Faith			
Fame			
Friendships			
Fun			
Growth			
Happiness			
Harmony			
Honesty			
Humor			
Influence			
Inner Harmony			
Justice			
Kindness			
Knowledge			

Leadership			
Learning			
Love			
Loyalty			
Meaningful			
Openness			
Optimism			
Peace			
Pleasure			
Poise			
Power			
Popularity			
Positivity			
Practicality			
Recognition			
Religion			
Reputation			
Respect			
Responsibility			
Security			
Self-Respect			
Service			
Spirituality			
Stability			
Success			
Status			
Trustworthiness			
Wealth			
Wisdom			
Work			

www.ingramcontent.com/pod-product-compliance
Lightning Source LLC
LaVergne TN
LVHW091327150826
845673LV00006B/1796

* 9 7 9 8 8 8 7 7 2 9 9 5 4 *